Langenscheidt

Scientific English
für Mediziner und Naturwissenschaftler

Wortschatz und Formulierungshilfen für wissenschaftliche Publikationen und Vorträge

von Christian Hrdina und Robert Hrdina

Langenscheidt

Berlin · München · Wien · Zürich · New York

Bibliografische Information Der Deutschen Bibliothek
Die Deutsche Bibliothek verzeichnet diese Publikation in der Deutschen
Nationalbibliografie; detaillierte bibliografische Daten sind im Internet über
http://dnb.ddb.de abrufbar.

*Eingetragene (registrierte) Warenzeichen sowie Gebrauchsmuster und Patente
sind in diesem Wörterbuch nicht ausdrücklich gekennzeichnet. Daraus kann
nicht geschlossen werden, dass die betreffenden Bezeichnungen frei sind oder
frei verwendet werden können.*

*Das Werk ist urheberrechtlich geschützt. Jede Verwendung außerhalb der
Grenzen des Urheberrechtsgesetzes bedarf der vorherigen schriftlichen
Zustimmung des Verlages. Dies gilt besonders für Übersetzungen,
Vervielfältigungen, auch von Teilen des Werkes, Mikroverfilmungen,
Bearbeitungen sonstiger Art sowie für die Einspeicherung in elektronische
Systeme.*

© 2006 Langenscheidt Fachverlag GmbH München
Gesamtherstellung: Druckhaus „Thomas Müntzer" GmbH, Bad Langensalza/Thüringen
Printed in Germany
ISBN-13: 978-3-86117-257-4
ISBN-10: 3-86117-257-7

Table of contents — Inhaltsübersicht

Vorwort — 6

Benutzerhinweise — 8

I. Written publications — Schriftliche Publikationen

A. Introduction — Einführung

A 1. Aim of the study	Ziel der Studie	11
A 2. Subject of the study	Gegenstand der Studie	13
A 3. What is new?	Was ist neu?	17

B. Materials and methods — Material und Methodik

B 1. Study type and methods	Studienart und Methodik	19
B 2. Statistical analysis	Statistik	23
B 3. Patient population	Patientenkollektiv	26
B 4. Ethical committee	Ethikkommission	30

C. Results — Ergebnisse

C 1. Listing results	Ergebnisse anführen	32
C 2. Quantities (Basics)	Mengenangaben (Grundlagen)	36
C 3. Links to tables and figures	Verweis auf Tabellen und Abbildungen	40

D. Discussion — Diskussion

D 1. How to mention	Erwähnungen	42
D 2. How to describe	Beschreibungen	45

D 3. How to enumerate	Aufzählungen	47
D 4. How to give examples	Beispiele	49
D 5. How to emphasize	Betonungen und Hervorhebungen	51
D 6. How to compare and contrast	Vergleiche und Gegenüberstellungen	54
D 7. How to present development and change	Entwicklungen und Tendenzen	58
D 8. How to evaluate	Wertung und Beurteilung	60
D 9. How to refer to the literature	Vergleich mit Literatur	62
D 9.1. Results of other studies	Ergebnisse anderer Studien	62
D 9.2. Common ground	Gemeinsamkeiten	64
D 9.3. Differences	Unterschiede	66
D 10. How to argue	Beweisführung	68
D 10.1. Causal analysis	Ursachenanalyse	68
D 10.2. How to argue for s.th.	Pro	72
D 10.3. How to argue against s.th.	Contra	75
D 10.4. How to draw conclusions	Schlussfolgerungen	77
D 11. How to explain relations	Zusammenhänge	79
D 12. How to assume	Vermutungen	83
D 13. How to express opinions	Meinungen	85
D 14. How to use quantities (advanced)	Mengenangaben (weiterführend)	87
D 15. How to integrate aspects of time	Zeitliche Angaben	92
D 16. How to analyse details	Detailanalyse	94
D 17. How to point out problems and limitations	Probleme und Limitierungen der Studie	96

E Summary	Zusammenfassung	**97**
F Acknowledgements	Danksagungen	**99**

II. Oral presentation / Vorträge

1. How to welcome and guide the audience	Begrüßung und Moderation	**102**
2. Introduction	Einleitung	**104**
3. How to link up passages	Überleitungen	**106**
4. Slides, transparencies and graphics	Dias, Folien und grafische Elemente	**109**
5. How to emphasize	Hervorhebungen	**113**
6. Summary / Closing remarks	Zusammenfassung / Schlusswort	**114**
7. How to invite the audience to ask questions	Aufforderung zu Fragen	**116**
8. How to answer and retort	Antwort auf Fragen, Anmerkungen und Einwände	**118**
9. How to ask and comment	Fragen und Kommentare anbringen	**123**

Appendix 1	How to submit / Manuskripteinsendung	**127**
Appendix 2	Comparison AE/BE / Vergleich AE/BE	**132**
Appendix 3	Glossary / Glossar	**135**

Vorwort

Wer kennt das Problem nicht: Nach monate- oder gar jahrelanger Forschungsarbeit haben Sie vielversprechende Ergebnisse erzielt, die Sie möglichst schnell einem internationalen Fachpublikum zugänglich machen wollen. Schon lange wissen Sie, auf welchen Kongressen Sie Ihre Arbeit präsentieren möchten und welches Journal das geeignete Forum für eine Publikation wäre. Und schon lange ist Ihnen eines klar: Egal, was Sie mitzuteilen haben, es muss auf Englisch sein.
Mühsam und zeitraubend wird Satz für Satz konstruiert, immer wieder müssen Sie im Wörterbuch nachschlagen, und wenn endlich ein Absatz zu Papier gebracht ist, wirkt er doch streckenweise sprachlich unbeholfen und eintönig. Formulieren Sie Ihren Vortrag komplett aus und lernen ihn auswendig, oder sind Sie routiniert genug, um in freier Rede mit korrektem Englisch aufzutreten? Kündigen Sie Ihre Dias regelmäßig mit dem Ausspruch *Here you can see ...* an? Bedienen Sie sich aus einem breiten Repertoire an englischen Ausdrucksweisen oder erschöpft sich Ihr angelerntes Englisch in festgefahrenen Redewendungen und rigiden Satzbauten?

Hier setzt unser Buch an mit dem Ziel, dem wissenschaftlichen Autor eine praktische und reichhaltige Formulierungshilfe zu bieten.
Auf der Basis mehrerer hundert medizinisch-naturwissenschaftlicher Artikel aus renommierten englischsprachigen Fachzeitschriften entstand dieses praxisorientierte Handbuch, das über 500 für das Scientific English essenzielle Begriffe und rund 900 universell anwendbare, authentische Satzbeispiele anschaulich präsentiert. Dabei werden auf dem internationalen wissenschaftlichen Publikationssektor unerfahrene und routinierte Fachautoren gleichermaßen angesprochen.

Der Aufbau von **Teil I Written publications – Schriftliche Publikationen** orientiert sich an der Standardgliederung eines wissenschaftlichen Artikels, so dass das Buch kontextbezogen während des gesamten Schreibvorgangs herangezogen werden kann. Es wurde versucht, typische und wiederkehrende Aspekte deskriptiven und argumentativen Schreibens möglichst umfassend abzubilden. Fundamentale Bereiche wie Aufzählungen und Vergleiche werden ebenso behandelt wie die Präsentation, Analyse, Abgrenzung und Diskussion eigener Forschungsergebnisse.
Analog werden im **Teil II Oral presentation – Vorträge** verschiedene situative Aspekte eines wissenschaftlichen Vortrags in gebrauchsfertigem Englisch dargeboten.

Im Anhang finden sich Formulierungsvorschläge für Anschreiben an Herausgeber wissenschaftlicher Fachzeitschriften im Rahmen der Manuskripteinsendung, ein Vergleich zwischen American English (AE) und British English (BE) sowie ein deutsch-englisches Glossar für Teil I.

Anders als zahllose Werke, die sich mit konzeptionellen und formalen Aspekten eines wissenschaftlichen Essays befassen, dient dieses Buch als unmittelbare Schreib- und Formulierungshilfe und verzichtet bewusst auf theoretische Abhandlungen über die

Planung und Entstehung einer wissenschaftlichen Publikation. Dabei handelt es sich ausdrücklich nicht um ein Fachwörterbuch; Fachausdrücke aus der Medizin und naturwissenschaftlichen Disziplinen werden nur exemplarisch im Zusammenhang mit Beispielsätzen verwendet.

Wir wünschen allen Benutzern unbeschwertes und produktives Arbeiten mit unserem Buch, genügend Mut und Experimentierfreude im Umgang mit Scientific English und das nötige Glück auf dem Weg zur perfekten englischen Publikation.

Die Autoren danken Herrn Prof. Dr. med. Joachim Sciuk, Herrn Dr. Philip A. Luelsdorff und Herrn Dr. Manfred Eichhorn für die eingehende Begutachtung des Manuskripts und ihre fachlichen Ratschläge. Dank gilt ferner Gray Kochhar-Lindgren, PhD, für den langjährigen linguistischen Gedankenaustausch.

Augsburg und Regensburg, im Oktober 2005

Christian Hrdina, Robert Hrdina

Benutzerhinweise

Scientific English für Mediziner und Naturwissenschaftler gliedert sich in **Teil I Written publications – Schriftliche Publikationen** und **Teil II Oral presentation – Vorträge**.

Der Aufbau von Teil I folgt der Standardgliederung eines medizinisch-naturwissenschaftlichen Artikels, um ein möglichst zeitsparendes, kontextbezogenes Nachschlagen benötigter Begriffe zu ermöglichen.

Am Beginn jedes Kapitels wird das jeweilige Basisvokabular dargeboten (**blaue Schrift**). Im Anschluss folgen weiterführende Begriffe (Aufbauvokabular; **schwarze Schrift**) mit Variationen des Basisvokabulars, sowie zahlreiche englische Satzbeispiele zu den verwendeten Begriffen (siehe Schema).

Diese authentischen Beispielsätze können unmittelbar in die eigene wissenschaftliche Arbeit übernommen und thematisch adaptiert werden.

Längere Abschnitte mit Aufbauvokabular und Satzbeispielen gliedern sich in übersichtliche Einheiten, die den Erfordernissen des jeweiligen Kapitels angepasst sind (z.B. Zusammenfassung von Synonymen, Sortierung nach auf- bzw. absteigenden Kriterien, Gruppierung von Gegensatzpaaren etc.).

Werden mehrere englische Begriffe mit gleich lautender deutscher Übersetzung dargeboten, so sind diese synonym verwendbar. Im Falle semantischer Unterschiede zwischen solchen Vokabeln wird explizit darauf hingewiesen.

Sie werden einigen Vokabeln mehrfach beggnen, da diese für verschiedene Kapitel gleichermaßen von Relevanz sind.

In Teil II werden – sortiert nach unterschiedlichen Sprechsituationen – mehr als 250 vollständige und universell verwendbare Formulierungen für wissenschaftliche Vorträge in englischer Sprache dargeboten. Hierbei wurde auf eine separate Vokabelliste bewusst verzichtet.

Auf Unterschiede im British English (BE) und American English (AE) wird an geeigneter Stelle hingewiesen. Teil II folgt durchweg der britischen Schreibweise, ebenso das deutsch-englische Glossar.

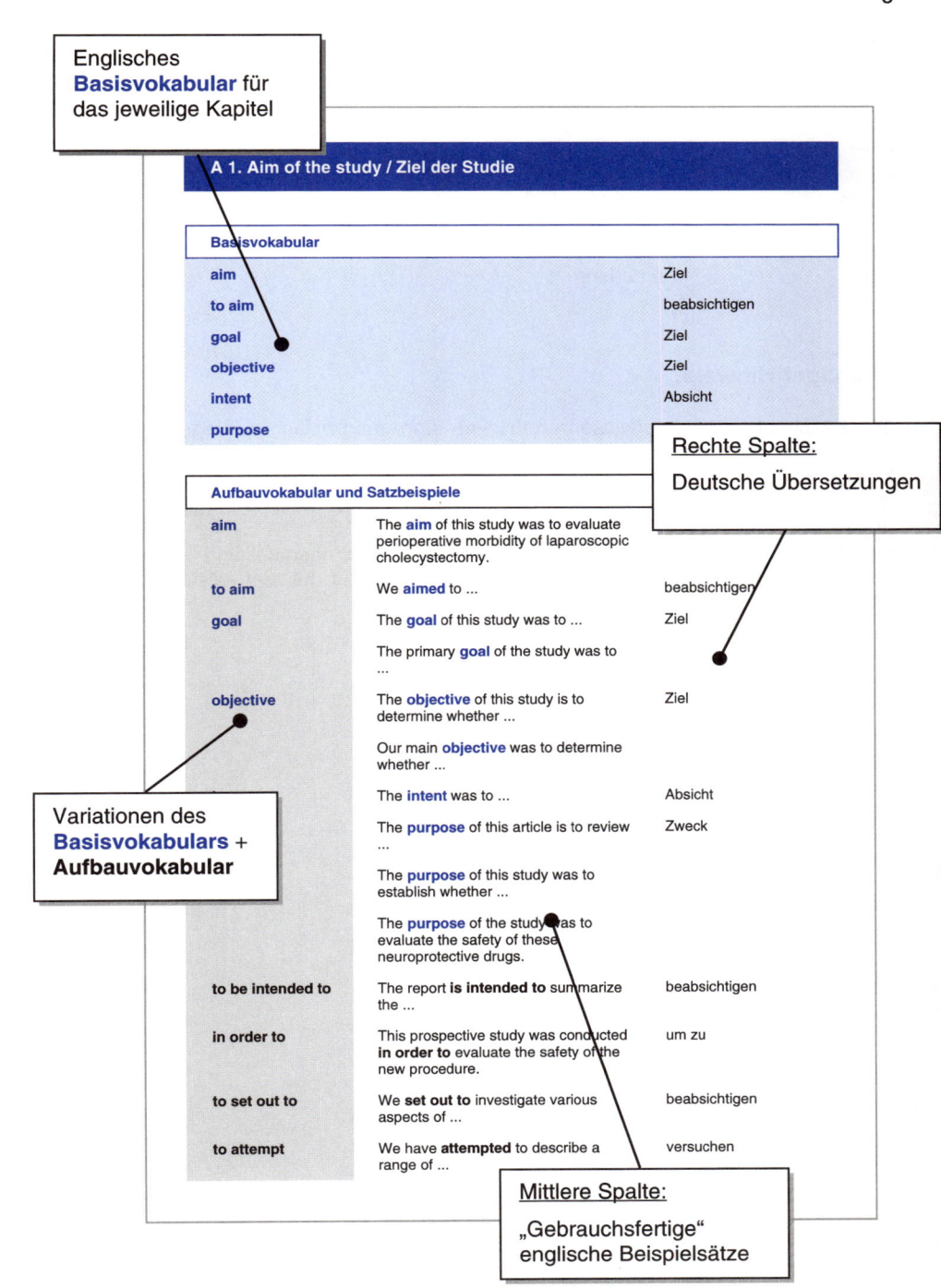

Englisches **Basisvokabular** für das jeweilige Kapitel

A 1. Aim of the study / Ziel der Studie

Basisvokabular

aim	Ziel
to aim	beabsichtigen
goal	Ziel
objective	Ziel
intent	Absicht
purpose	

Rechte Spalte: Deutsche Übersetzungen

Aufbauvokabular und Satzbeispiele

aim	The **aim** of this study was to evaluate perioperative morbidity of laparoscopic cholecystectomy.	
to aim	We **aimed** to ...	beabsichtigen
goal	The **goal** of this study was to ...	Ziel
	The primary **goal** of the study was to ...	
objective	The **objective** of this study is to determine whether ...	Ziel
	Our main **objective** was to determine whether ...	
	The **intent** was to ...	Absicht
	The **purpose** of this article is to review ...	Zweck
	The **purpose** of this study was to establish whether ...	
	The **purpose** of the study was to evaluate the safety of these neuroprotective drugs.	
to be intended to	The report **is intended to** summarize the ...	beabsichtigen
in order to	This prospective study was conducted **in order to** evaluate the safety of the new procedure.	um zu
to set out to	We **set out to** investigate various aspects of ...	beabsichtigen
to attempt	We have **attempted** to describe a range of ...	versuchen

Variationen des **Basisvokabulars** + **Aufbauvokabular**

Mittlere Spalte: „Gebrauchsfertige" englische Beispielsätze

Abkürzungsverzeichnis

AE	American English
BE	British English
etw.	etwas
i.S.v.	im Sinne von
jmdm.	jemandem
jmdn.	jemanden
s.b.	somebody
s.th.	something

Wichtiger Hinweis:

Die beschriebenen naturwissenschaftlichen und medizinischen Begebenheiten und Zahlenangaben stellen nicht in allen Fällen reelle Tatsachen dar und dienen nur zur Veranschaulichung eines sprachlichen Sachverhalts. Entsprechende Angaben können nicht als Grundlage für wissenschaftliche und medizinische Arbeit jeglicher Art herangezogen werden.
Verwendete Personen- und Institutsnamen sowie Zeitschriftentitel sind frei erfunden und besitzen lediglich Beispielcharakter. Jegliche Ähnlichkeit mit real existierenden Personen, Instituten und Medien ist rein zufällig.

I. Written publications / Schriftliche Publikationen

A Introduction / Einführung

A 1. Aim of the study / Ziel der Studie

Basisvokabular	
aim	Ziel
to aim	beabsichtigen
goal	Ziel
objective	Ziel
intent	Absicht
purpose	Zweck

Aufbauvokabular und Satzbeispiele		
aim	The aim of this study was to evaluate perioperative morbidity of laparoscopic cholecystectomy.	Ziel
to aim	We aimed to ...	beabsichtigen
goal	The goal of this study was to ...	Ziel
	The primary goal of the study was to ...	
objective	The objective of this study is to determine whether ...	Ziel

Ziel der Studie

	Our main **objective** was to determine whether ...	
intent	The **intent** was to ...	Absicht
purpose	The **purpose** of this article is to review ...	Zweck
	The **purpose** of this study was to establish whether ...	
	The **purpose** of the study was to evaluate the safety of these neuroprotective drugs.	
to be intended to	The report **is intended to** summarize the ...	beabsichtigen
in order to	This prospective study was conducted **in order to** evaluate the safety of the new procedure.	um zu
to set out to	We **set out to** investigate various aspects of ...	beabsichtigen
to attempt	We have **attempted** to describe a range of ...	versuchen

A 2. Subject of the study / Gegenstand der Studie

Basisvokabular

study	Studie
survey	Erhebung, Übersicht, Überblick
review	*hier:* Übersichtsarbeit
article	Artikel
report	Bericht
essay	Essay, Fachaufsatz
analysis	Analyse
work	Arbeit
investigation	Untersuchung
research	Forschung

Aufbauvokabular und Satzbeispiele

to perform **(a study)**	This **study** was **performed** in order to measure the increase in atmospheric carbon dioxide concentration.	eine Studie durchführen
to conduct **(a study)**	The Association of Abdominal Surgeons **conducted** a prospective **study** of 1,518 patients who underwent gastrectomy. Here we **conduct** an extensive investigation of ...	eine Studie durchführen

Gegenstand der Studie

survey	A national **survey** was therefore **conducted** to broadly estimate the frequency of major complications associated with this technique. This **survey** was **conducted** between January 2001 and June 2002.	Erhebung, Übersicht, Überblick
to present review	This **review** presents ... The authors **present** the potential of ... Here we **present** new evidence that ...	präsentieren, vorstellen *hier:* Übersichtsarbeit
to address s.th.	This **study addresses** the question in a more structured way.	etw. ansprechen
to describe article	In this **article** we **describe** ...	beschreiben Artikel
report	This **report describes** the results of ...	Bericht
to illustrate	This pictorial **essay** describes and **illustrates** heat flux anomalies in Antarctica over the past ten years.	illustrieren, veranschaulichen
to review s.th.	This **article reviews** the aetiologies and imaging findings of acute mesenteric ischemia. In this **article**, the CT findings of acute mesenteric ischemia are **reviewed**.	einen Überblick geben über etw.

Gegenstand der Studie

to investigate s.th.	The current **analysis** **investigated** the hypothesis that ...	untersuchen
analysis		Analyse
essay	In this **essay**, we have tried to **investigate** ...	Essay, Fachaufsatz
to examine	Our **work examines** ...	untersuchen
work		Arbeit
to explore	Throughout this **analysis** we **explore** the structure of bacterial outer membrane lipoproteins.	erforschen, untersuchen
to test	The purpose of the **study** was to **test** the clinical feasibility and utility of a new scanning protocol.	testen, prüfen
to determine	This **study** was performed to **determine** differences in electron dynamics.	feststellen, bestimmen
	A portion of this **study** was dedicated to **determining** whether any time difference was noticeable between the two technologies.	
to evaluate s.th.	In our **investigation**, we **evaluated** ...	einschätzen, beurteilen, bewerten
investigation		Untersuchung

Gegenstand der Studie

to assess s.th.	In our **research**, we **assessed** ...	einschätzen, beurteilen, bewerten
		Info: **to evaluate** *und* **to assess** *werden hier synonym gebraucht. Bei der Auswertung von Ergebnissen wird nur* **to evaluate results** *verwendet.*
research		Forschung
question of interest	Yet another **question of interest** for us was ...	von Interesse
concern	Of additional **concern** has been the value of satellite magnetic data.	Belang
to concern oneself with s.th.	In this **study**, we **concerned ourselves with** the impact that this method had on climate prediction.	sich mit etw. befassen
to offer insight into s.th.	This **investigation offers insight into** ...	Einblick in etw. gewähren
to compare s.th. with s.th.	This **investigation compared** ... **with** ...	etw. mit etw. vergleichen
to settle a question	This **study settles the** important **question** of whether laser dissection or cautery is better for the removal of the gall bladder from the hepatic bed.	eine Frage (eindeutig/endgültig) beantworten

A 3. What is new? / Was ist neu?

Basisvokabular

new	neu
novel	neuartig

Aufbauvokabular und Satzbeispiele

new	What is **new** is ...	neu
	We report a **new** method of ...	
	Here we propose a **new** technique ...	
	We have developed a **new** technology to assess ...	
	Here we present **new** evidence that ...	
novel	We report a **novel** process of ...	neuartig
for the first time	Here we report/show/demonstrate/present **for the first time** that ...	zum ersten Mal, erstmalig
	The observation reported here provides **for the first time** key insight into ...	
	For the first time, we believe (to be able) to shed light on ...	

Was ist neu?

> **Info:** *Die folgenden Beispielsätze beinhalten kein neues Vokabular. Sie stellen lediglich weitere themenbezogene Formulierungsmöglichkeiten dar.*

Here we describe a hitherto ignored phenomenon, namely ...

Unlike many of our predecessors, we ...

Our results challenge previous claims that ...

Altogether, these results bring **new** constraints to models for ...

So far, this procedure has been limited to ...

Here we present a model that goes much further.

B Materials and methods / Material und Methodik

B 1. Study type and methods / Studienart und Methodik

Basisvokabular	
data	Daten
questionnaire	Fragebogen
respondent	Befragter
rate of return	Rücklaufquote
response rate	Antwortrate
study protocol	Studienprotokoll
method	Methode
supplementary information	(Informations-)Beilage
follow-up	Follow-Up, Nachbeobachtung
period	Zeitraum

Aufbauvokabular und Satzbeispiele		
data	**Data** was summarized with regard to overall morbidity, mortality, length of hospital stay, and duration of postoperative recovery.	Daten
	The **data** summarized in this review represent the initial experience with genomic sequencing.	*Info:* **Data** *kann im Englischen sowohl im Singular als auch im Plural verwendet werden.*

Studienart und Methodik

to express data	All **data** are **expressed** as mean values ± 1 standard deviation.	Daten angeben
available	Reliable **data** was **available** for 162 probes.	verfügbar, zur Verfügung stehen
questionnaire	The **questionnaire** was structured to focus on major procedure-related injuries. We have designed the **questionnaire** as follows: ...	Fragebogen
respondent	A total of 413 **respondents** have submitted valuable data.	Befragter
rate of return	They provided an adequate **rate of return**.	Rücklaufquote
response rate	The **response rate** was 68%.	Antwortrate
to provide	1,200 institutions **provided** specific numerical **data**.	liefern
to submit	A total of 45 institutions **submitted** prospective **data** from September 1990 to August 1992.	zur Verfügung stellen, einreichen
to query	Mortality was not specifically **queried**.	erfragen
study protocol	The **study protocol** included the acquisition of 2-dimensional echocardiography to evaluate regional wall motion.	Studienprotokoll
method	We have applied the subsequent **methods**: ...	Methode

Studienart und Methodik

to retrieve	All CT scans of the upper cervical region performed between April and November 1999 were **retrieved** for study.	heranziehen
to record	The Swedish surgical registry prospectively **recorded** 1,164 appendectomies during the years 1991–1993.	verzeichnen, aufzeichnen
to screen (for)	Patients were **screened for** the presence of free intraperitoneal gas.	bezüglich etw. untersuchen, auf etw. hin untersuchen
to monitor	Our aim was to **monitor** hypocentral stresses in the earthquake.	beobachten, aufzeichnen
to measure	Leukocyte counts were **measured** in the same week that the scintigraphy was performed.	messen
supplementary information	Protein purification is described in the **Supplementary Information**. Proteins were incubated for 30 minutes as recommended by ... (see **Supplementary Information**). For further details of the incubation procedure see **Supplementary Information**.	(Informations-)Beilage *Info:* **Supplementary Information** *wird dann groß geschrieben, wenn diese Journalbeilage explizit so betitelt ist.*
follow-up	On **follow-up** at 6 mo, 3 patients had severe restenosis of the infarct-related vessel.	Follow-Up, Nachbeobachtung
to follow s.th. up	Our plan is to **follow** this population **up** for a several-year period.	etw. nachbeobachten
period	This study was conducted over a several-year **period**.	Zeitraum

Studienart und Methodik

to collect data about s.th.	We **collected data about** marine mammal mortality in the Baltic Sea. **Data** was **collected** prospectively.	Daten erheben über etw.
to gather information about s.th.	The main focus of this **study** was to **gather information about** the procedure-related morbidity after endoscopic sphincterotomy.	Informationen gewinnen über etw.
to gain knowledge of s.th.	The objective has been to **gain knowledge of** the mechanisms ...	Kenntnis erlangen über etw.
to obtain s.th.	We have **obtained data** about 1,245 consecutive cases.	etw. erhalten, gewinnen

B 2. Statistical analysis / Statistik

Basisvokabular

significance	Signifikanz
significant	signifikant
to test	testen
to calculate	berechnen
to analyse (BE) **to analyze (AE)**	analysieren
to evaluate	einschätzen, beurteilen, bewerten
to assess	einschätzen, beurteilen, bewerten
to determine	bestimmen
to compare	vergleichen
to examine	untersuchen

Aufbauvokabular und Satzbeispiele

significant	A probability P value of less than 0.05 was considered **significant**.	signifikant
	P < 0.05 was considered to indicate a statistically **significant** difference.	
	These differences were not statistically **significant**.	

Statistik

significance	The reduction in the conversion rate between the two laparoscopic groups from 5.2 to 1.8% was statistically **significant**.	
	The hypothesis that ... was examined by **using** the χ^2-test for trend, with **significance** assigned at the 5% level.	Signifikanz
to test	Waste-water was **tested** for ...	testen
to use (a test)	The χ^2-test was **used** to **calculate** the difference ...	(einen Test) verwenden
to calculate		berechnen
to analyse (BE)	The χ^2-test was **used** to **analyse (BE)/analyze (AE)** the difference ...	analysieren
to analyze (AE)		
to test	The χ^2-test was **used** to **test** the difference ...	testen
to evaluate	The χ^2-test was **used** to **evaluate** the difference in sensitivity.	einschätzen, beurteilen, bewerten
to assess	The χ^2-test was **used** to **assess** the difference ...	einschätzen, beurteilen, bewerten

> *Info:* **to evaluate** *und* **to assess** *werden hier synonym gebraucht. Bei der Auswertung von Ergebnissen wird nur* **to evaluate results** *verwendet.*

to determine	The χ^2-test was **used** to **determine** the difference ...	bestimmen
to perform (a test)	The χ^2-test was **performed** to **evaluate** the difference ...	durchführen

Statistik

to compare	The χ^2-test was **performed** to **compare** the sensitivity of ...	vergleichen
to employ (a test)	We **employed** the χ^2-test to **analyse (BE)/analyze (AE)** whether ...	*hier:* (einen Test) anwenden
to examine	The hypothesis that ... was **examined** by **using** the χ^2-test statistic.	untersuchen
	The differences among groups for the variables studied were **evaluated** by analysis of variance.	
to perform	Analysis was **performed** (by) using *Softwarename* (*Softwarefirma, Firmensitz*).	durchführen
	Statistical calculations were **performed** (by) using a statistical software package (*Softwarename 1 und Softwarename 2, Softwarefirma, Firmensitz*).	
	All statistical analyses described above were **performed** (by) using the software program *Softwarename* (*Softwarefirma, Firmensitz*).	
to process	All **data** were **processed** using *Softwarename* (*Softwarefirma, Firmensitz*).	verarbeiten

B 3. Patient population / Patientenkollektiv

Basisvokabular

inclusion	Einschluss
exclusion	Ausschluss
patient population	Patientenpopulation, Patientenkollektiv
sample	Stichprobe
cohort	Kohorte, Reihe (von Probanden)
series	Reihe, Serie
subject	Gegenstand, Thema *hier:* Person
individuals	Individuen

Aufbauvokabular und Satzbeispiele

inclusion criterion **exclusion criterion**	**Inclusion** and **exclusion criteria** were defined by an expert panel.	Ein- und Ausschlusskriterium
sample	Small **sample** size resulted from strict **exclusion criteria**.	Stichprobe
	The patient **sample included** 28 men and 97 women.	
to include	The study **included** 108 patients.	einschließen
	58 patients were **included**.	

Patientenkollektiv

patient population	The **patient population** included 54 consecutive patients.	Patientenpopulation, Patientenkollektiv
to exclude	Patients were **excluded** in the case of ...	ausschließen
to comprise	The series **comprised** two groups of patients who ...	einschließen
to consist of	The **patient population consisted of** 108 patients with ...	sich zusammensetzen aus
to enlist	Five consecutive patients were **enlisted** from the acute trauma service.	einschließen, rekrutieren
to enrol series	A **series** of 187 patients was **enrolled**.	einschließen, rekrutieren Reihe, Serie
to select	For the study, 46 patients were **selected**.	auswählen
patient selection	**Patient selection** in this retrospective analysis was biased/biassed.	Patientenauswahl *Info: Beide Schreibweisen sind gebräuchlich.*
to recruit	The patients **recruited** for this study showed ...	rekrutieren
cohort	A **cohort** of 108 patients was **recruited**.	Kohorte, Reihe (von Probanden)
recruitment criteria	**Recruitment criteria** were: ...	Auswahlkriterien
to participate (in s.th.)	Six healthy male volunteers **participated in** this study.	teilnehmen (an etw.)
to take part (in s.th.)	46 patients with osteoarthritis **took part in** this investigation.	teilnehmen (an etw.)

Patientenkollektiv

to group	The series were **grouped** into either single-centre or multicentre (BE)/multicenter (AE) reviews.	gruppieren; *hier:* in Kategorien einteilen
	We **grouped** patients with unilateral renal artery stenosis of 50–75% and patients with unilateral renal artery stenosis greater than 75%.	
group	Two **groups** of patients were formed and divided into five **subgroups** each.	Gruppe
subgroup		Untergruppe
to randomise (BE)	40 **subjects** were **randomised (BE)/randomized (AE)** to group A and 40 to group B.	randomisiert zuteilen
to randomize (AE)		
subject		*hier:* Person
to classify (as)	The patient was **classified as** severely injured if ...	klassifizieren, einstufen (als)
to define (as)	Three groups of patients were **defined**: ...	definieren (als)
age	Mean patient **age** was 61 years (range 21–88 years).	Alter
	The **age** of the patients ranged from 8 to 98 years.	
	The patients averaged 47 years of **age**.	
total	The series included a **total** of 12,397 patients.	Gesamtheit, Gesamtzahl
	Of this **total**, 758 patients were treated at academic hospitals and 504 at private institutions.	
in total	**In total**, 342 blood samples were tested for traces of ...	insgesamt

Patientenkollektiv

overall

Overall, 700 **subjects** were tested for symptoms of ...

insgesamt

An **overall** of 500 **individuals** took part in ...

Gesamtheit, Gesamtzahl

individuals

Individuen

B 4. Ethical committee / Ethikkommission

Basisvokabular

ethical committee	Ethikkommission
approval	Zustimmung
informed consent	aufgeklärtes Einverständnis

Aufbauvokabular und Satzbeispiele

to approve	The investigational review board **approved** the study.	zustimmen (i.S.v. absegnen, genehmigen)
		Info: Im Zusammenhang mit einem Genehmigungsverfahren sollte **to approve s.th.** verwendet werden. Das umgangssprachlich gelegentlich synonym gebrauchte **to approve of s.th.** bedeutet soviel wie „Gefallen finden an etw." und zieht nicht notwendigerweise die offizielle Erteilung einer Studiengenehmigung nach sich.
informed consent	All candidates gave written **informed consent**, and the study was **approved** by the institutional review board.	aufgeklärtes Einverständnis
	This study was **approved** by the committee on human research. Written **informed consent** was not required.	

Ethikkommission

ethical committee approval	**Informed consent** and **ethical committee approval** <u>was</u> obtained.	Ethikkommission Zustimmung
	Institutional review board **approval** and **informed** patient **consent** <u>were</u> obtained.	*Info:* Beide Formen (Singular/Plural) sind gebräuchlich. Bevorzugt sollte **were** verwendet werden.
to endorse s.th.	The **ethical committee endorsed** the study design prior to patient acquisition.	zustimmen, gutheißen *Info:* Synonym zu **to approve s.th.**
	The **ethical committee** of our institution **endorsed** the study protocol.	
	The protocol was **endorsed** by the **ethical committee** of our institution and each subject gave **informed** written **consent**.	
to waive	**Informed consent** was **waived**.	verzichten auf
exemption (from)	This investigation met the criteria for an **exemption from** institutional review board **approval**.	Ausnahme (von), Freistellung (von)
to require	Neither institutional board **approval** nor **informed consent** were **required**.	erfordern

C Results / Ergebnisse

C 1. Listing results / Ergebnisse anführen

Basisvokabular

result	Resultat, Ergebnis
finding	Ergebnis, Schluss
outcome	Ergebnis
to find	(heraus)finden, zu einem Ergebnis kommen
to observe	beobachten
to encounter s.th.	etw. begegnen, auftreten (etw. tritt auf)
rate	Häufigkeit, Rate
frequency	Häufigkeit
incidence	Inzidenz
gamut	Bandbreite, Spektrum
scale	Bandbreite, Spektrum
to range from ... to ...	von ... bis ... reichen
to vary from ... to ...	von ... bis ... variieren

Ergebnisse anführen

Aufbauvokabular und Satzbeispiele

result	Our study has yielded the following **results**: ...	Resultat, Ergebnis
finding	The main **finding** of this study is that 98% of the patient population showed the same symptoms after succinylcholine had been administered.	Ergebnis, Schluss
	We have encountered contradictory **findings**.	
outcome	All the applied pharmaceuticals led to the same **outcome**.	Ergebnis
to find	We **found** abnormal prion strains in more than 29% of the samples.	(heraus)finden, zu einem Ergebnis kommen
	The highest endothelin-1 concentrations were **found** in the four patients with injury-severity scores of more than 40.	
	The remaining 5 patients were **found** to have gallstones.	
to observe	Instantaneous vaporization was **observed** in 8 of 63 different settings.	beobachten
to encounter s.th.	Amyloid fibrils were **encountered** in 109 probes.	etw. begegnen, auftreten (etw. tritt auf)
to see **to be seen**	Septic shock was **seen** in 14 patients.	beobachten auftreten
to come across s.th.	When analysing the final data, we **came across** three major aberrations.	auf etw. stoßen, begegnen
to detect	We **detected** a significant deviation from the mean value.	feststellen, entdecken

Ergebnisse anführen

to identify	Significant deviations were **identified** in 1,586 probes.	feststellen
to reveal	Overall, 55 gastroduodenal perforations were **revealed**.	feststellen, sich zeigen
to be present	Wound infections **were present** in more than one third of all patients.	auftreten
to occur	All 15 deaths **occurred** among the 2,360 patients older than 65 years.	auftreten
	This phenomenon **occurred** in 0.14%.	
occurrence	Specific queries included the frequency of injury to the aorta and the **occurrence** of any delayed complications.	das Auftreten
evidence of s.th.	There was **evidence of** biotic loss in the ecosystem observed.	Nachweis von etw.; *hier:* etw. wurde nachgewiesen
rate	The mean **rate** of vessel injury was 0.6%.	Häufigkeit, Rate
	The technique is associated with low **rates** of morbidity and mortality.	
frequency	Intracranial bleeding occurred with a **frequency** of 14%.	Häufigkeit
incidence	Patients treated for acute cholecystitis had an **incidence** of postoperative complications of 17.1%.	Inzidenz
	The **incidence** of bile duct injury in the first 90 patients was 2.2%, as compared with 0.1% for subsequent patients.	

to stand at	The death **rate** in this unselected series **stands at** 0.5%.	sich belaufen auf
to represent	This **represents** a mortality rate of 0.6% in this group.	darstellen, entsprechen
gamut	The reported injuries ran the whole **gamut** of severe traumatic lesions.	Bandbreite, Spektrum
scale	The **scale** of antibiotics **ranged from** ... **to** ...	Bandbreite, Spektrum
to range from ... to ...	Mortality rates **ranged from** 0.5% **to** 1.0%.	von ... bis ... reichen
	Mortality from this disorder remains high, **ranging from** 70% **to** 90%.	
to vary from ... to ...	Contemporary rates of contamination **vary from** 0% **to** 0.4% and are often cited at 0.1% to 0.25%.	von ... bis ... variieren
	The sensitivity **varied from** 62% **to** 44%.	
respectively	The **incidence** of major bile duct injury, vessel injury and overall morbidity was 0.3%, 0.4% and 4% **respectively**.	beziehungsweise

C 2. Quantities (Basics) / Mengenangaben (Grundlagen)

Basisvokabular

many	viele
a number of	eine Reihe (von)
a score of	eine Reihe (von)
some	manche
a few	ein paar, einige
few	wenige
little	wenig *(bei nicht zählbaren Dingen)*
high	hoch
low	niedrig
rate	Rate
percentage	Prozentsatz, prozentualer Anteil
proportion	Anteil, Verhältnis
part	Teil
partial	teilweise
fraction	Bruchteil
half of	die Hälfte von
one third/quarter of	ein Drittel/Viertel von
majority	Mehrheit

Mengenangaben (Grundlagen)

minority	Minderheit
all (of)	alle, alles
none (of)	niemand, nichts
total	gesamt, komplett, Gesamtheit
in total	zusammen, alles in allem
overall	insgesamt, Gesamt-

Aufbauvokabular und Satzbeispiele

many	**Many** aspects of bacterial fermentation deserve further investigation.	viele
a number of	**A number of** previous studies have used ventilation scans as a clinical tool.	eine Reihe (von)
a score of	**A score of** surveys have reported ...	eine Reihe (von)
some	**Some** experts claim that ...	manche
a few	We could isolate only **a few** samples of ...	ein paar, einige
few	**Few** institutions have so far adopted the new technique.	wenige
little	Technical aspects were of **little** interest to us.	wenig *(bei nicht zählbaren Dingen)*
high	The **high** number of ... is explained by ...	hoch
low	Total organic carbon was relatively **low**.	niedrig

Mengenangaben (Grundlagen) 38

Info: Die nebenstehenden Beispielsätze beinhalten kein neues Vokabular. Sie stellen lediglich weitere themenbezogene Formulierungsmöglichkeiten dar.	**20% of** the prion strains showed signs of ... **In 20% of** the events, we observed signs of ... **In** 97 **of** the 118 cases, ... **Of** the 25 patients studied, 4 had a history of previous myocardial infarction.	
rate	The method is generally associated with a low **rate** of postoperative morbidity.	Rate
percentage	A high **percentage** of these complications can be attributed to ...	Prozentsatz, prozentualer Anteil
proportion	A significantly lower **proportion** of dolphins showed signs of brevetoxin inhalation in group 1 than in group 2.	Anteil, Verhältnis
part	Intraoperative bleeding accounted for the smallest **part** of all complications.	Teil
partial	The amino-terminal region is **partially** responsible for converting soluble protein into amyloid fibres (BE)/fibers (AE).	teilweise
fraction	A tiny **fraction** of the overall population, namely 0.3%, showed minor complications.	Bruchteil
half of	More than **half of** the patient population suffered from severe abdominal injury.	die Hälfte von

Mengenangaben (Grundlagen)

one third of	Nonetheless, more than **one third of** the reported deaths were attributable to a technical complication.	ein Drittel von
majority	The **majority** of wildlife species in Bolivia show/shows ...	Mehrheit
minority	Only a **minority** of the analysed (BE)/analyzed (AE) samples was/were ...	Minderheit

> *Info:* **Majority/minority** *kann sowohl im Singular als auch im Plural gebraucht werden.*

all (of)	**All** samples were evaluated for ...	alle, alles
	All of the molecules had ...	
none (of)	**None of** the mycoparasites had ...	niemand, nichts
total	A **total** of 7,604 splenectomies was reported.	gesamt, komplett, Gesamtheit
in total	**In total**, 57 large vessels were injured.	zusammen, alles in allem
overall	**Overall**, the most common complication was ...	insgesamt, Gesamt-
	Overall, 55 gastroduodenal perforations were revealed.	
	They described an **overall** morbidity rate of 4.5%.	

C 3. Links to tables and figures / Verweis auf Tabellen und Abbildungen

Basisvokabular	
table	Tabelle
figure	Abbildung
diagram	Diagramm

Info: Die Beispielsätze dieses Kapitels sind prinzipiell auf jede der o.g. **Basisvokabeln** *anwendbar.*

Aufbauvokabular und Satzbeispiele		
table	Between 1991 and 1998 complication rates decreased from 8.3 to 4.1% (**Table** 5).	Tabelle
to show	**Table** 2 **shows** ...	zeigen
figure	The field intensity variations are **shown** in **Figure** 4.	Abbildung
	The relationship of perfusion distribution to lung water distribution is **shown** in **Figure** 7 by combining the data from Figures 4 and 6.	
to list	**Table** 2 **lists** ...	auflisten
	Brevetoxin concentrations in seagrass are **listed** in **Table** 1.	

Verweis auf Tabellen und Abbildungen

to give	**Table** 5 **gives** the most frequent alternative diagnoses encountered.	*hier:* zeigen, darbieten
	Table 5 **gives** the estimated sensitivities of each imaging technique.	
	The estimates of site temperature changes are **given** in **Tables** 2 and 3.	
to present	**Table** 3 **presents** ...	präsentieren, zeigen
	Results of kinetic analysis are **presented** in **Table** 1.	
to report	Clinical, pathological and imaging data are **reported** in **Table** 1.	*hier:* darlegen
to indicate	The types of intravenous contrast media used are **indicated** in **Table** 4.	aufzeigen
to demonstrate	**Figure** 5 **demonstrates** a focus of increased activity in the inferior pole of the right thyroid lobe.	demonstrieren, zeigen
to highlight	**Diagram** 4 **highlights** the recent development in ...	hervorheben, verdeutlichen
diagram		Diagramm
to reflect	This development is **reflected** in **Table** 2.	widerspiegeln

to summarize	**Table** 2 **summarizes** the differences in protein coding genes between the two parasites.	zusammenfassen
	Table 1 and 2 **summarize** ...	
to combine	**Table** 4 **combines** the findings of the two studies.	*hier:* zusammenfügen
to compare	**Figure** 2 **compares** bacterial growth in various soil types.	vergleichen

D Discussion / Diskussion

D 1. How to mention / Erwähnungen

Basisvokabular

to name	nennen, anführen
to mention	erwähnen, bemerken
to observe	beobachten, feststellen
to perceive	bemerken, wahrnehmen
to encounter s.th.	etw. begegnen, auftreten (etw. tritt auf)
to detect	entdecken, feststellen
to report	berichten, erwähnen
to reveal	aufdecken, feststellen
to disclose	aufdecken, bekannt machen

Aufbauvokabular und Satzbeispiele

to name	Of the many different aspects associated with the use of sedatives, we would like to **name** the following: …	nennen, anführen
to mention	In this context, one has to **mention** the extraordinary impact of the new technique on patients' acceptance.	erwähnen, bemerken
	The significantly shorter incubation time should also be **mentioned** here.	

Erwähnungen

to observe	We have **observed** a significant decrease of non-surgical complications like thrombosis, pneumonia or myocardial infarction. This was **observed** despite the fact that ...	beobachten, feststellen
to perceive	It has been **perceived** that all tested proteins showed a rapid increase in fluorescence.	bemerken, wahrnehmen
to encounter s.th.	Bowel injuries were **encountered** in 109 patients.	etw. begegnen, auftreten (etw. tritt auf)
to detect	We have **detected** symptoms of inflammation in 29 of 413 patients.	entdecken, feststellen
to report	We **report** the results of a multicentre (BE)/multicenter (AE) survey among German university hospitals between 1991 and 1998.	berichten, erwähnen
to reveal	A closer examination **revealed** that these amide stacks stabilize the macromolecular aggregates.	aufdecken, feststellen
to disclose	The prospective type of registration tends to **disclose** minor faults and omit major ones.	aufdecken, bekannt machen
to consider	**Considering** the large and widely distributed nature of the sample, these results provide ... Other issues worth **considering** are ...	bedenken, erwägen
to take into consideration	The staggering acceptance of this new treatment by the patient population must also be **taken into consideration**.	in Erwägung ziehen, in Betracht ziehen

Erwähnungen

to take into account	**Taking** this **into account**, the total scanning time may be considered to be 5 min.	in Erwägung ziehen, in Betracht ziehen
to acknowledge	One should **acknowledge** the fact that ...	bedenken, anerkennen

D 2. How to describe / Beschreibungen

Basisvokabular

to describe	beschreiben
to illustrate	illustrieren, verdeutlichen
to delineate	schildern, plakativ darstellen
to depict	darstellen
to scrutinize	unter die Lupe nehmen
to specify	verdeutlichen

Aufbauvokabular und Satzbeispiele

to describe	This pictorial essay **describes** the use of multislice helical CT.	beschreiben
to illustrate	These studies **illustrate** the effectiveness of the novel method for monitoring breast cancer patients for recurrent disease.	illustrieren, verdeutlichen
to delineate	The following paragraph **delineates** in great detail the different steps of the procedure.	schildern, plakativ darstellen
to depict	Figure 7 **depicts** the effects of the new agent on blood pressure and heart rate.	darstellen
	The negative effect of hypobaric hypoxia on lowlanders at high altitude has long been known and variously been **depicted** by numerous scientists worldwide.	

Beschreibungen

to scrutinize	Smith et al. **scrutinized** the correlation between these two parameters in 1994.	unter die Lupe nehmen
to specify	This idea is best **specified** by the following example: ...	verdeutlichen

D 3. How to enumerate / Aufzählungen

Basisvokabular

first, ...	Erstens ...
firstly, ...	*Info:* Bevorzugt wird hier die einfache Variante **First** verwendet.
first off, ...	
second, ...	Zweitens ...
third, ...	Drittens ...
furthermore	außerdem, darüber hinaus
moreover	außerdem, darüber hinaus
in addition	außerdem, darüber hinaus
besides	außerdem, darüber hinaus
finally	Schließlich ..., Letztlich ...

Aufbauvokabular und Satzbeispiele

first, ...	**First**, we would like to point out that ...	Erstens ...
firstly, ...	**Firstly**, we would like to point out that ...	
first off, ...	**First off**, we would like to point out that ...	
to begin with	**To begin with**, we would like to give a brief historical survey.	zunächst
then	**Then** it has to be mentioned that ...	dann

Aufzählungen

furthermore	**Furthermore**, a general sense of the magnitude of certain complications can be obtained from the treatment reported.	außerdem, darüber hinaus
moreover	**Moreover**, a general sense ...	außerdem, darüber hinaus
in addition	**In addition**, a general sense ...	außerdem, darüber hinaus
	In addition to the above, ...	
also	**Also**, the energy distributions measured by ... were ...	auch, außerdem
	The following statement is **also** true: ...	*Info:* **Also** *kann keinen verneinten Satz einleiten.*
other	**Other** issues worth considering are ...	andere(s), weitere(s)
another	**Another** important consideration is that most surgeons excluded high-risk individuals.	andere(s), weitere(s)
	The rise of virus-related deaths is **another** disturbing fact.	
besides	**Besides**, there are other advantages that deserve mentioning.	außerdem, darüber hinaus
	There are other previously unknown enzymes **besides** those mentioned above.	neben
finally	**Finally**, we may not forget ...	Schließlich ..., Letztlich ...
	Finally, it should be noted that ...	
the former / the latter	Group A showed a significantly lower rate of pulmonary embolism than group B. While **the former** received a high-dose treatment, **the latter** has only been treated according to the traditional low-dose protocol.	erstere(s) / letztere(s)

D 4. How to give examples / Beispiele

Basisvokabular

example	Beispiel
for example	zum Beispiel
for instance	zum Beispiel
e.g.	zum Beispiel
like	wie etwa, wie z.B.
such as	wie etwa, wie z.B.

Aufbauvokabular und Satzbeispiele

example	This is an excellent **example** of the potential power of this technology.	Beispiel
for example	Pike, **for example**, are freshwater predators.	zum Beispiel
	In one case, **for example**, a multitrauma patient was taken directly to the operating room due to the severe nature of his injuries.	
for instance	Bile duct injury, **for instance**, increased by more than 10% from 1991 to 1998.	zum Beispiel
e.g.	In the course of our analysis we have detected a variety of pitfalls, **e.g.** lack of patient compliance.	zum Beispiel *Info: Die anzuführende Beispielkomponente steht immer <u>nach</u> e.g.*
like	Advantages **like** higher resolution and shorter scanning times are obvious.	wie etwa, wie z.B.

Beispiele

such as | Other procedures, **such as** sonography and intravenous cholangiography, have been widely accepted. | wie etwa, wie z.B.

> *Info:* **Such as** *zieht i.d.R. mehrere Beispielkomponenten nach sich und wird vornehmlich im BE verwendet.* **Like** *hingegen ist hier universell verwendbar.*

D 5. How to emphasize / Betonungen und Hervorhebungen

Basisvokabular

to emphasize	betonen
to stress	betonen
to point out	hinweisen (auf)
to foreground	hervorheben
to highlight	hervorheben
to underline	unterstreichen
above all	vor allem
particular	besonders
considerable	beträchtlich
remarkable	bemerkenswert
important	wichtig

Aufbauvokabular und Satzbeispiele

to emphasize	It is important to **emphasize** that ...	betonen
to stress	The authors would like to **stress** the importance of ...	betonen
to point out	We have to **point out** that any study of this kind is subject to various limitations.	hinweisen (auf)
to foreground	Of 20 related cases we have chosen to **foreground** the following two.	hervorheben

Betonungen und Hervorhebungen

to highlight	In this context it is indispensable to **highlight** the achievements of ancient Chinese medicine.	hervorheben
	These figures seem very high, and it is tempting to think that only the most extreme cases have been **highlighted**.	
to underline	Smith et al. have **underlined** the essential role of ...	unterstreichen
to underscore	The tragic situation in Mexico **underscored** the inefficiency of ...	unterstreichen, betonen
above all	**Above all**, we must not forget ...	vor allem
	Above all, the aim of such a forum should be to provide the best possible service to children and their families.	
particular	Of **particular** concern is the role of ...	besonders
in particular	**In particular**, it was a widespread opinion that ...	insbesondere
particularly	Ebola is a **particularly** nasty form of ...	besonders
	The results of our study support this theory, **particularly** when we take a closer look at ...	
considerable	There is **considerable** research interest in new treatments.	beträchtlich
remarkable	We note that there is **remarkable** intersubject variability in ...	bemerkenswert
important	Most **important**, in our study, no new sites of metastases were seen on scanning after therapy.	wichtig

Betonungen und Hervorhebungen

special	These findings suggest that the deposition of coating material deserves **special** attention.	besonders, besondere(-n/-s)
impressive	The most **impressive** thing about this report is the fact that ...	beeindruckend
significant	The most **significant** outcome gleaned from the data in this study is the ...	*hier:* bedeutend; signifikant
essential	For many decades, penicillin has been the **essential** anti-infective drug.	essenziell, wesentlich
critical	Rising ozone levels have played a **critical** role in ...	*hier:* entscheidend, tragend
crucial	The patient has entered a **crucial** stage of his illness.	entscheidend, gravierend (*stärker als* **critical**)
vital	Our data reveal the **vital** role of ... in this novel concept.	lebenswichtig, *hier:* alles entscheidend
paramount	Immediate imaging of the affected vessels is of **paramount** importance. This has turned out to be **paramount** in treating malignant melanoma patients.	alles entscheidend, herausragend

D 6. How to compare and contrast / Vergleiche und Gegenüberstellungen

Basisvokabular

to compare (with)	vergleichen (mit)
to distinguish (between)	unterscheiden (zwischen)
to differentiate (between)	differenzieren (zwischen)
to contrast	gegenüberstellen
on the contrary	im Gegenteil
opposed to	im Gegensatz zu
on the one hand	einerseits
on the other hand	andererseits
however	jedoch, hingegen
yet	dennoch

Aufbauvokabular und Satzbeispiele

to compare (with)	The side-effects of AIDS wasting may be **compared with** …	vergleichen (mit)
	The results of our study **compare** favourably (BE)/favorably (AE) **with** those reported in the literature.	
	The major drawback of the laparoscopic procedure relates to its apparent higher bile duct injury rate **compared with** the open procedure.	

Vergleiche und Gegenüberstellungen

	The incidence of hepatic injury in the first 100 patients was 2.0%, (as) **compared with** 1.0% for subsequent patients.	
in comparison	**In comparison**, the readmission rates in two series of conventional cholecystectomies were 3 and 5 percent.	im Vergleich (dazu)
comparable	These findings are **comparable** to the 0.5% incidence of bile duct injury observed in the prospective multicentre (BE)/multicenter (AE) study of the Southern Surgeons Club.	vergleichbar

> **Info:** Streng genommen bedeutet **comparable**, dass sich Dinge zwar vergleichen lassen, aber nicht notwendigerweise ähnlich sein müssen. Im Sprachgebrauch wird **comparable** aber häufig synonym zu **similar** verwendet (s. Beispielsatz). *Similar* ist in diesem Falle eigentlich bevorzugt zu verwenden.

similar	These findings are **similar** to those of Smith et al.	ähnlich
	In a **similar** fashion, the data set from the chest and abdomen may be used to reformat a CT angiogram of the aorta.	
identical	Complication rates were **identical** for both groups.	identisch, gleich
to differentiate (between)	Previous studies did not **differentiate between** high-dose and low-dose therapy.	differenzieren (zwischen)
to distinguish (between)	We have to **distinguish between** patient-related and external factors.	unterscheiden (zwischen)

Vergleiche und Gegenüberstellungen

to make a distinction (between)	We have to **make an** important **distinction between** the African and the Asian virus type.	eine Unterscheidung treffen (zwischen)
unlike	**Unlike** previous publications, our research aimed at ...	anders als
to contrast	Our aim was to **contrast** non-invasive and surgical therapies.	gegenüberstellen
on the contrary	**On the contrary**, it seems beneficial to group A.	im Gegenteil
contrary to	**Contrary to** the widely held belief that ...	entgegen, im Gegensatz zu
in contrast to	This experience stands **in contrast to** concerns raised in the media.	im Widerspruch zu
contradictory	Others have reported **contradictory** findings.	widersprechend, gegenteilig
opposed to	In this analysis, the definition of "academic" as **opposed to** "private practice" surgeons was based on ...	im Gegensatz zu
on the one hand / **on the other hand**	**On the one hand**, the new procedure has rapidly spread in western countries. **On the other hand**, it has turned out to be irresponsibly expensive.	einerseits / andererseits
whereas	It has been stated that paramedics in the United States tend to conduct onsite emergency surgery, **whereas** their European counterparts prefer traditional hospital care.	wogegen

Vergleiche und Gegenüberstellungen

however	Its clinical value, **however**, has been the subject of intense debate. **However**, there was a high proportion of minor injuries.	jedoch, hingegen
yet	**Yet**, there are certain alarming aspects to consider. **Yet** unlike influenza, for example, SARS shows ...	dennoch
nonetheless	**Nonetheless**, CT is still not available around the clock in many facilities.	dennoch, trotzdem
nevertheless	Despite its decreasing popularity, this method is **nevertheless** very effective.	dennoch, trotzdem
despite	**Despite** previously reported advances in nanotechnology, there are still ...	trotz
in spite of	**In spite of** previously ...	trotz

D 7. How to present development and change / Entwicklungen und Tendenzen

Info: Entwicklungen und Veränderungen quantitativer Größen werden im Kapitel D14 ausführlich behandelt.

Basisvokabular

development	Entwicklung
tendency	Tendenz
to increase	zunehmen
to decrease	abnehmen
to improve	(sich) verbessern
to deteriorate	(sich) verschlechtern

Aufbauvokabular und Satzbeispiele

development	This article illustrates the latest **developments** in evolutionary biology.	Entwicklung
tendency	These data show a clear **tendency** towards the use of ...	Tendenz
to increase	Drivers who rely on airbag protection alone **increase** their fatality risk exponentially.	zunehmen
to decrease	Complication rates have **decreased** since 1994.	abnehmen

Entwicklungen und Tendenzen

to increase by **to decrease by**	This **increased/decreased** the risk of major complications **by** 10%.	erhöhen um, steigern um erniedrigen um, mindern um
to improve	Far from being optimistic, we have to admit that the overall situation has slightly **improved**. However, routine intraoperative cholangiography may **improve** the intraoperative recognition of bile duct injury.	(sich) verbessern
to enhance	Sanitary systems in these countries will have to be **enhanced** significantly before ...	*hier:* verbessern; *auch:* fördern, steigern, verstärken
to deteriorate	The situation in Vietnam is **deteriorating**.	(sich) verschlechtern
to exacerbate	Rheumatic gonarthritis can be **exacerbated** by bacterial superinfection.	verschlechtern, verschärfen

D 8. How to evaluate / Wertung und Beurteilung

Basisvokabular

to evaluate	einschätzen, beurteilen, bewerten
to assess	einschätzen, beurteilen, bewerten
to estimate	schätzen, abschätzen *(nur bei messbaren/ quantifizierbaren Größen)*
to under-/ overestimate	unter-/überschätzen

Aufbauvokabular und Satzbeispiele

to evaluate	The aim of our study was to **evaluate** the effects of hyperthermia on tumour (BE)/tumor (AE) growth.	einschätzen, beurteilen, bewerten
to assess	In our research, we **assessed** ...	einschätzen, beurteilen, bewerten
		Info: **to evaluate** *und* **to assess** *werden hier synonym gebraucht. Bei der Auswertung von Ergebnissen wird nur* **to evaluate results** *verwendet.*
to assess s.th. for s.th.	Novel alpha-fetoprotein agonists were **assessed** in immortalized cell lines **for** their ability to enhance radioresistant DNA synthesis.	etw. auf etw. hin beurteilen

Wertung und Beurteilung

assessment	With any new procedure, there must be critical **assessment** of the related complications.	Bewertung
to estimate	Without reliable data, the true complication rates can only be **estimated**.	schätzen, abschätzen
	Estimated figures range from ... to ...	
estimate	Due to a lack of reliable data, the figures obtained are a rough **estimate** at best.	Schätzung

Info: **Estimate** *sollte immer dann verwendet werden, wenn es um numerische Schätzungen geht.* **Estimation** *wird häufig synonym gebraucht, bezeichnet streng genommen aber jegliche Art der Einschätzung (z.B. auch einer Situation).*

to regard s.th. as s.th.	Only five years ago the method was **regarded as** the gold-standard in pain treatment.	etw. für etw. halten/erachten
to consider s.th. (to be) s.th.	Obesity was initially **considered (to be)** a contraindication to the new procedure.	etw. für etw. halten/erachten
	This was **considered (to be)** unnecessary because of the obvious advantages of the new method.	
to believe **s.th. is believed to be ...**	The intramural air in small bowel ischemia **is believed to be** a result of mucosal injury.	etw. für etw. halten/erachten
to deem s.th. (as) s.th.	Due to these deficiencies in previous studies, we **deem** their findings **(as)** not representative.	etw. für etw. halten/erachten *(sehr förmlich)*

D 9. How to refer to the literature / Vergleich mit Literatur

D 9.1. Results of other studies / Ergebnisse anderer Studien

Info: Da die nachfolgenden Vokabeln für dieses Kapitel von gleichrangiger Bedeutung sind, wird auf eine Unterteilung in Basis- und Aufbauvokabular verzichtet.

to find	Smith et al. **found** that ...	feststellen, finden
to show	A recent study by Smith et al. **showed** ...	zeigen
to report	It remains a highly morbid disorder with **reported** mortality rates of 40%.	berichten, dokumentieren
	Several large published series have **reported** their initial experience with ...	
to note	Other series have **noted** post-operative bile leak rates of 0.2% to 2.0%.	verzeichnen
to cite	Single and multi-institutional experiences have **cited** rates of 0% to 2%.	verzeichnen
to describe	The method has been **described** by several authors with varying reported success.	beschreiben
	Previous studies **describe** an overall morbidity rate of ...	

to demonstrate	Previous experience has **demonstrated** that ...	demonstrieren, zeigen
	Some authors have **demonstrated** that ...	
	A previous report by Moore and colleagues in a cohort of 24 patients **demonstrated** good agreement between the two methods.	
to indicate	Previous studies have **indicated** that ...	anzeigen, hinweisen
to suggest	Others have **suggested** that ...	*hier:* vorbringen
to claim	Several authors have **claimed** that ...	behaupten
comparison study	Several **comparison studies** have proven that ...	Vergleichsstudie, Vergleichsarbeit

Vergleich mit Literatur

D 9.2. Common ground / Gemeinsamkeiten

Basisvokabular

to correlate with	korrelieren mit
to correspond with	entsprechen
to be consistent with	übereinstimmen mit
in accordance with	in Übereinstimmung mit
in agreement with	in Übereinstimmung mit
concordant with	übereinstimmend/ konkordant mit
in line with	in Übereinstimmung mit
in keeping with	in Übereinstimmung mit

Aufbauvokabular und Satzbeispiele

to correlate with	These results **correlate** well **with** the literature.	korrelieren mit
to correspond with	A major morbidity rate of 2% **corresponds with** the overall complication rates of 2% to 11% that have been reported.	entsprechen
to be consistent with	Our results **are consistent with** those reported by Smith et al. Our results **are consistent with** a recent study ...	übereinstimmen mit
in accordance with	This observation is **in accordance with** Smith et al. (2), who reported ...	in Übereinstimmung mit

Gemeinsamkeiten

in agreement with	**In agreement with** the findings in previous studies, we found that ...	in Übereinstimmung mit
	These results are **in** close **agreement with** those obtained by Moore et al.	
concordant with	Our data is **concordant with** those of previous studies.	übereinstimmend/ konkordant mit
in line with	Our results are **in line with** data from the literature.	in Übereinstimmung mit
in keeping with	These results are **in keeping with** previous studies, which reported that ...	in Übereinstimmung mit
s.th. compares favourably (BE)/ favorably (AE) with s.th.	These results **compare favourably (BE)/favorably (AE) with** those reported in the literature.	etw. ist gut mit etw. vergleichbar *i.S.v.:* nicht abweichen von
comparable	This review of available data on rainfall and drought frequency reveals **comparable** results.	vergleichbar
similar	**Similar** findings were reported by ... Many studies have reported **similar** results.	ähnlich

> **Info:** Streng genommen bedeutet **comparable**, dass sich Dinge zwar vergleichen lassen, aber nicht notwendigerweise ähnlich sein müssen. Im Sprachgebrauch wird **comparable** aber häufig synonym zu **similar** verwendet (s. Beispielsatz). **Similar** ist in diesem Falle eigentlich bevorzugt zu verwenden.

Vergleich mit Literatur

D 9.3. Differences / Unterschiede

Info: Vgl. hierzu Kapitel D6.

Basisvokabular

different	anders, unterschiedlich
to take a different view (on)	eine unterschiedliche Haltung einnehmen
to differ from	sich unterscheiden von
to deviate (from)	abweichen (von)
to vary (from)	abweichen (von)
to contradict	widersprechen
contradictory	widersprechend, gegenteilig
in contrast to	im Gegensatz zu
to disagree	nicht zustimmen, anderer Meinung sein

Aufbauvokabular und Satzbeispiele

different	Earlier studies have reported **different** results.	anders, unterschiedlich
	Several recent studies with the same or closely related methods have come to very **different** conclusions.	
to take a different view (on)	Smith et al. **take a different view on** the importance of ...	eine unterschiedliche Haltung einnehmen

Unterschiede

to differ from	Our findings **differ from** previously recorded data.	sich unterscheiden von
	The number of severe injuries did not **differ from** that reported by others.	
to deviate (from)	Initial figures **deviate** to a large extent **from** data gathered during a recent simulation despite unaltered parameters.	abweichen (von)
to vary (from)	The results of recent multicentre (BE)/multicenter (AE) studies strongly **vary from** those obtained in 1998.	abweichen (von)
to contradict	One feels tempted to categorically **contradict** all findings in the 1992 study.	widersprechen
contradictory	Comparison studies have reported **contradictory** findings.	widersprechend, gegenteilig
in contrast to	**In contrast to** U.S. standards we have chosen to abide by the standard values set by European researchers.	im Gegensatz zu
	In contrast to these earlier findings we observed ...	
to disagree (with)	As far as our Asian control group's findings are concerned we strongly **disagree with** the way these results have been obtained.	nicht zustimmen, anderer Meinung sein

D 10. How to argue / Beweisführung

D 10.1. Causal analysis / Ursachenanalyse

Basisvokabular

because of	wegen, aufgrund von, weil, ...
caused by	verursacht von, begründet durch
to result from	resultieren aus
to originate from	herrühren von
to stem from	herrühren von
due to	wegen, aufgrund von
owing to	wegen, aufgrund von
to relate to	bedingt sein durch, abhängen von (*auch:* zusammenhängen mit)
to attribute to	zurückführen auf
attributable to	zurückzuführen auf
as a consequence	folglich

Aufbauvokabular und Satzbeispiele

because of	It is **because of** negligence in sanitary matters that diseases like cholera are on the rise.	wegen, aufgrund von, weil, ...

Ursachenanalyse

caused by	The increase in lethal cases of cholera is **caused by** ...	verursacht von, begründet durch
to result from	Such strictures may **result from** inflammation and fibrosis due to bile leak.	resultieren aus
	Eighteen of 33 postoperative deaths **resulted from** operative injury.	
to originate from	The higher number of wound infections **originates from** the preselection of patients in group B.	herrühren von
to stem from	This widespread view **stems from** a fatal misinterpretation of basic conditions.	herrühren von
due to	This may be **due to** increased levels of ...	wegen, aufgrund von
owing to	**Owing to** the ongoing depletion of natural resources, alternative ways of generating electricity will play a crucial role.	wegen, aufgrund von
to relate to	The major drawback of this technique **relates to** its apparently higher costs.	bedingt sein durch, abhängen von (*auch:* zusammenhängen mit)
	These changes **relate to** a number of factors, including patient convenience and lower costs.	
	A significant proportion of operative deaths are **related to** technical complications.	

Ursachenanalyse

to attribute to	No complications were **attributed** directly **to** laser-surgical techniques.	zurückführen auf
	The differences in remission rates between our study and the previous survey can be **attributed to** differences in study design.	
	This fact might also be **attributed**, in part, **to** ...	
attributable to	Nonetheless, more than half of the reported deaths were **attributable to** a technical complication.	zurückzuführen auf
as a consequence	**As a consequence**, we chose a different approach.	folglich
apparent	The advantages of method A are **apparent**.	offensichtlich
obvious	It is **obvious** that the same vaccines frequently show different results in different patients.	offensichtlich
evident	The advantages of the new concept are **evident**: ...	offensichtlich, auf der Hand liegend
clear	It is **clear** that ...	eindeutig, klar
	The reasons for this increase are not made **clear** by the present study.	
multifactorial	The high mortality is **multifactorial**, but it is often related to a delay in diagnosis.	multifaktoriell

Ursachenanalyse

to combine (to)	These factors **combine to** significantly improve image quality.	zusammenwirken
to contribute to	The late recognition of these injuries in patients with sepsis and peritonitis **contributes to** the relatively high associated mortality.	beitragen zu, bedingen
to explain	Biased selection **explains** the differences between ...	erklären
to be explained (by)	The increase **is explained by** ...	sich erklären (durch)
explanation	Possible **explanations** for the differences are ...	Erklärung
responsible (for)	Bacteria are partially **responsible for** the anaerobic decomposition of sludge.	verantwortlich (für)
therefore	It is **therefore** imperative for us to use ... **Therefore**, it is imperative ...	deswegen, deshalb
hence	...; **hence**, it is imperative, that we use ...	deswegen, deshalb
for this reason	**For this reason**, we decided to form three subgroups.	aus diesem Grund
that is (the reason) why ...	**That is the reason why** this vicious form of Ebola is still on the rise.	deswegen, aus diesem Grund, darum

Pro

D 10.2. How to argue for s.th. / Pro

Basisvokabular

to show	zeigen
to indicate	hinweisen auf
to demonstrate	zeigen, demonstrieren
to prove	beweisen, bestätigen
to support	unterstützen
to confirm	bestätigen, bekräftigen
to corroborate	bekräftigen, untermauern (*stärker als* **to confirm**)
to provide an argument for s.th.	ein Argument für etw. liefern
to provide support for s.th.	Unterstützung bieten
to advocate	befürworten
to endorse	befürworten, gutheißen *auch:* absegnen i.S.v. genehmigen

Aufbauvokabular und Satzbeispiele

to show	This study clearly **shows** that there is no difference in the safety of this procedure whether it is performed in an academic or a private hospital. In summary, our results clearly **show** that …	zeigen

Pro

to indicate	Our experience **indicated** that the thinner-section reconstructions are redundant. These results **indicate** that ...	hinweisen auf
to demonstrate	This study **demonstrates** a marked increase in the frequency of ... These data **demonstrate** that laparoscopic appendectomy is essentially a safe procedure.	zeigen, demonstrieren
to prove	These findings **prove** our hypothesis of ... Our research has **proven** that ...	beweisen, bestätigen
ample evidence	We believe to have gathered **ample evidence** to verify our theory.	ausreichende Beweise
to support	The existence of a learning curve for the novel method is clearly **supported** by this study. The findings of this study **support** the assumption that ...	unterstützen
to confirm	This review **confirms** previously held notions, such as ... This study has **confirmed** the presence of a wide range of ... Our data **confirm** and expand previous observations.	bestätigen, bekräftigen
to corroborate	Our data **corroborate** the trend towards minimally-invasive techniques in gallstone surgery.	bekräftigen, untermauern (*stärker als* **to confirm**)
to provide an argument for s.th.	These results **provide** a strong **argument for** ...	ein Argument für etw. liefern

Pro

to provide support for s.th.	These studies **provide support for** the hypothesis that ...	Unterstützung bieten
to advocate	This approach can be most strongly **advocated** when symptoms are poorly localized.	befürworten
to endorse	These guidelines have been **endorsed** by the following institutions: ...	befürworten, gutheißen *auch:* absegnen i.S.v. genehmigen
to be in favour (BE)/favor (AE) of s.th.	Our team **is in favour (BE)/favor of (AE)** a more restricted use of the novel method.	für etw. sein
to favour (BE)/favor (AE) s.th.	We clearly **favour (BE)/favor (AE)** the Scandinavian solution.	befürworten, favorisieren
to approve of s.th.	The Society for ... has **approved of** the recommendation to ...	befürworten, begrüßen

> *Info:* Im Zusammenhang mit einem Genehmigungsverfahren sollte **to approve s.th.** *verwendet werden* (The Ethical Committee has **approved** the study protocol).

to lend countenance to	We therefore **lend countenance to** a more widespread use of ...	billigen, unterstützen

D 10.3. How to argue against s.th. / Contra

Basisvokabular

to criticize	kritisieren
to disagree	nicht einverstanden sein
to be against s.th.	gegen etw. sein
to disapprove of s.th.	etw. missbilligen, nicht befürworten
to object to s.th.	etw. ablehnen, widersprechen
to reject s.th.	etw. ablehnen, zurückweisen
to disprove s.th.	etw. widerlegen

Aufbauvokabular und Satzbeispiele

to criticize	This model has been **criticized** in many recent publications.	kritisieren
to disagree (with)	Based upon the results of this study we **disagree** with previously published recommendations ...	nicht einverstanden sein
to be against s.th.	For the above-mentioned reasons we **are against** a renaissance of metformin.	gegen etw. sein
to disapprove of s.th.	We therefore **disapprove of** the conventional technique that is still practised (BE)/practiced (AE) in many smaller community hospitals.	etw. missbilligen, nicht befürworten

Contra

to object to s.th.	As our results demonstrate an obvious advantage of the laser technique, we **object to** a continued use of the conventional device.	etw. ablehnen, widersprechen
to reject s.th.	On the basis of our data, we have to **reject** Meyer's theory.	etw. ablehnen, zurückweisen
to disprove s.th.	The conclusions drawn from previous studies are **disproven** by our results.	etw. widerlegen
to harbour (BE)/ harbor (AE) doubts about s.th.	We **harbour (BE)/harbor (AE)** some **doubts about** the validity of these data.	Zweifel an etw. hegen
to raise doubts about s.th.	These data **raise doubts about** ...	Zweifel an etw. aufwerfen
to raise concern about s.th.	These data **raise concern about** ...	Bedenken bezüglich etw. aufwerfen
to raise questions about s.th.	These data **raise questions about** ...	Fragen über etw. aufwerfen
to question s.th.	As a result of our findings, we **question** the widespread model of ...	etw. in Frage stellen
to challenge s.th.	The classic model was first **challenged** when...	etw. in Frage stellen (*stärker als* **to question s.th.**)

Info: Die folgenden Beispielsätze beinhalten kein neues Vokabular. Sie stellen lediglich weitere themenbezogene Formulierungsmöglichkeiten dar.	The present data do **not support** this assumption. This trend in the results did **not support** our hypothesis. Our data do **not confirm** the efficacy of ...	*Vollständige Verneinung der positiv belegten Verben aus dem Kapitel* **D 10.2 How to argue for s.th.** *als Mittel der Gegenargumentation.*

D 10.4. How to draw conclusions / Schlussfolgerungen

Basisvokabular

to conclude	*hier:* schlussfolgern (*auch:* abschließend)
conclusion	Schlussfolgerung
in conclusion	*hier:* somit, folglich (*auch:* abschließend)
as a consequence	folglich
thus	folglich, deswegen
hence	deswegen
therefore	deswegen

Aufbauvokabular und Satzbeispiele

to conclude	We **conclude** that this technology offers a number of benefits to …	*hier:* schlussfolgern
	On the basis of the data from this study, we **conclude** that …	
	To **conclude**, we would like to mention …	abschließend
conclusion	The results of these studies are consistent with the following **conclusions**.	Schlussfolgerung
in conclusion	**In conclusion**, a significant decrease of complications could be achieved by using the new technique.	*hier:* somit, folglich (*auch:* abschließend)

Schlussfolgerungen 78

as a consequence	**As a consequence** of our findings, we recommend that ...	folglich
thus	**Thus**, the new procedure accounts for less complications than ...	folglich, deswegen
	Theory A has **thus** been proven correct.	
hence	...; **hence**, this assessment cannot be neglected.	deswegen
therefore	We **therefore** advocate systematic surgical training.	deswegen
to indicate	We believe that this study **indicates** that ...	zeigen, hinweisen auf
	A comparison of the results obtained after the first cycle and the completion of chemotherapy **indicated** a statistically significant difference in ...	
	These results **indicate** that ...	
	This study **indicates** that ...	
as a result	**As a result**, mortality was cut in half.	im Ergebnis

D 11. How to explain relations / Zusammenhänge

Basisvokabular

to be associated with	etw. mit sich bringen, mit etw. zusammenhängen
to be related to	zusammenhängen mit (*auch:* verursacht werden durch)
to be based on	basieren auf
to depend on	abhängen von
with respect to	im Hinblick auf, unter Berücksichtigung von
with regard to	im Hinblick auf
context	Zusammenhang
to influence	beeinflussen
to affect	beeinflussen

Aufbauvokabular und Satzbeispiele

to be associated with	Increasing age **is associated with** increasing risks of postoperative complications.	etw. mit sich bringen, mit etw. zusammenhängen
to be related to	The degree to which the image is degraded **is related to** a number of parameters.	mit etw. zusammenhängen (*auch:* verursacht werden durch)
	They provided detailed information on all complications **related to** the new treatment.	

Zusammenhänge

to be based on	The conclusions drawn in recent studies **are** not always **based on** facts.	basieren auf
to depend on	In this clinical setting, survival rates strongly **depend on** the time until coronary angioplasty is successfully completed.	abhängen von
independent of	**Independent of** the increasing number of AIDS-related deaths, governmental measures to prevent further infections are still delayed.	unabhängig von
together with	These fractures often occur **together with** splenic injuries.	zusammen mit
coupled with	These fractures often occur **coupled with** splenic injuries.	zusammen mit
along with	These fractures often occur **along with** splenic injuries.	zusammen mit
in conjunction with	These fractures often occur **in conjunction with** splenic injuries.	zusammen mit, in Verbindung mit
in tandem with	Reconstruction was programmed into the scanner prospectively where possible so that processing occurred **in tandem with** image collection.	gleichzeitig mit, parallel
to be accompanied by	The postoperative course **was accompanied by** serious complications in less than 2% of the operations.	begleitet werden von
in the absence of	**In the absence of** reliable data, any evaluation of this approach is rather difficult.	ohne, aufgrund fehlender, in Abwesenheit von

Zusammenhänge

with respect to	The technique can be further optimized **with respect to** its industrial use.	im Hinblick auf, unter Berücksichtigung von
	The results of method A compare favourably (BE)/favorably (AE) with those of method B **with respect to** mortality, complications, and length of hospital stay.	
	Patient selection **with respect to** age or gender did not affect the complication rate.	
in this respect	**In this respect**, antibody production is disadvantageous.	in dieser Hinsicht
in respect of	Therefore, this method has several advantages **in respect of** cost-effectiveness.	hinsichtlich
concerning	Therefore, this method has several advantages **concerning** cost-effectiveness.	hinsichtlich
with regard to	Data was summarized **with regard to** overall morbidity, mortality, length of hospital stay, and duration of postoperative recovery.	im Hinblick auf
context	In this **context**, our data demonstrate that intermolecular contacts can be modified by ...	Zusammenhang
regardless of	All subjects have shown identical reactions **regardless of** their age.	ungeachtet
in terms of	The advantages of endoscopic surgical procedures **in terms of** reduced postoperative pain have been readily apparent.	i.S.v. „was etw. angeht"
as for s.th.	**As for** photosynthesis, we found ...	was etw. angeht

Zusammenhänge

as far as s.th. is concerned	**As far as** photosynthesis **is concerned**, we found ...	was etw. angeht
bearing (on)	These restrictions had some **bearing on** our study design.	(geringe) Auswirkung (auf) (*auch:* Bezug zu)
to influence	The introduction of multislice CT has strongly **influenced** cardiac imaging procedures.	beeinflussen
to affect	We have yet to determine how ... **affects** marine wildlife.	beeinflussen
effect (on)	The long-term **effects** of waste disposal have not been thoroughly investigated.	Einfluss (auf), Auswirkung (auf)
impact (on)	These technical improvements had an **impact on** surgical strategies in seriously injured patients.	(starker) Einfluss (auf), (erhebliche) Auswirkung (auf)

D 12. How to assume / Vermutungen

Basisvokabular

to assume	annehmen, vermuten
assumption	Vermutung
to presume	annehmen, vermuten
to suppose	annehmen, davon ausgehen, der Ansicht sein
to suggest	*hier:* vermuten (lassen)
to estimate	schätzen
to under-/ overestimate	unter-/überschätzen

Aufbauvokabular und Satzbeispiele

to assume	The short hospital stay can be **assumed** to indicate the early resumption of normal activities.	annehmen, vermuten
assumption	Based on the **assumption** that ...	Vermutung
	The findings of this study support the **assumption** that ...	
to presume	We **presume** that these findings are closely related to ...	annehmen, vermuten
to suppose	We might **suppose** magnetic resonance imaging to be the dominating imaging modality of the new millennium.	annehmen, davon ausgehen, der Ansicht sein

Vermutungen

to suggest	The data **suggest** that ... It has been **suggested** that ...	*hier:* vermuten (lassen)
to estimate	We may confidently **estimate** 13.5% of the overall Nigerian population to suffer from ...	schätzen
to under-/ overestimate	The low operative mortality rate of 0.04% may **underestimate** the true mortality.	unter-/überschätzen

D 13. How to express opinions / Meinungen

Basisvokabular

opinion	Meinung
view	Ansicht
to maintain	behaupten
to claim	behaupten
to assert	behaupten
to contend	behaupten, verfechten

Aufbauvokabular und Satzbeispiele

In our opinion In our view	In our opinion/view, patients do not benefit from ...	Unserer Meinung nach Unserer Ansicht nach
To hold the view that ...	Other authors hold the view that ...	der Ansicht sein
to maintain	Smith et al. maintain that the procedure is cost-effective.	behaupten
to claim	We do not claim that ...	behaupten
to assert	We assert method B to be the primary choice for ...	behaupten
to contend	They contend that rising complications are due to ...	behaupten, verfechten
to be convinced (of s.th./that)	We are convinced of the superiority of the novel technique.	(von etw.) überzeugt sein
	We are convinced that the novel technique is going to replace its predecessor.	überzeugt sein(, dass ...)

Meinungen

It is my contention that ...	**It is my contention that** every patient presenting with nausea should ...	Meiner festen Überzeugung nach
In our experience ...	**In our experience**, magnetic resonance imaging does not provide any additional information in the setting of gastrointestinal bleeding.	Nach unserer Erfahrung
to believe	We **believe** that ...	glauben

D 14. How to use quantities (advanced) / Mengenangaben (weiterführend)

Basisvokabular

major	schwerwiegend, Haupt-, hauptsächlich
minor	gering
more	mehr
less	weniger
increase	Anstieg, Steigerung
decrease	Reduktion, Abfall
frequent	häufig
rare	selten, sporadisch
main	Haupt-, hauptsächlich
mainly	hauptsächlich
largely	überwiegend, größtenteils

Aufbauvokabular und Satzbeispiele

major	Lack of hygiene is a **major** contributing factor to …	schwerwiegend, Haupt-, hauptsächlich
minor	All complications were reported, even such **minor** ones as …	gering
more	**More** than half of the subjects received …	mehr

Mengenangaben (weiterführend)

less	**Less** than half of the samples showed signs of ...	weniger
	The postoperative course was accompanied by serious complications in **less** than 2% of the operations.	
increase	The **increase** in complication rates is attributed to ...	Anstieg, Steigerung
to increase	We have **increased** the energy efficiency of these batteries by 14%.	steigern, ansteigen
gain	There is a significant **gain** in sensitivity ...	Zugewinn, Anstieg
decrease	A significant **decrease** in trace element concentration occurred after ...	Reduktion, Abfall
to decrease	Thermal stability has **decreased** due to ...	abnehmen
decline	Recently, there has been a significant **decline** in such cases.	Abnahme
to decline	Nutrient supply **declines** rapidly in areas of ...	abnehmen, (ab)sinken
frequent	This was a **frequent** complication of the traditional technique.	häufig
frequently	Bile duct injury occurs more **frequently** among patients with acute cholecystitis.	häufig
frequency	The **frequency** of volcanic activity in the designated area is extremely low.	Häufigkeit
rare	One of the **rare** findings was ...	selten, sporadisch

Mengenangaben (weiterführend)

rarely	3 groups performed phlebography either **rarely** or not at all.	selten, sporadisch
slight	Bacterial cell density showed only a **slight** difference after ...	geringfügig
slightly	A **slightly** higher incidence of ...	
marginal	Deviation from the set value was **marginal**.	geringfügig, marginal, *auch:* zu vernachlässigen
marginally	A **marginally** higher rate of ...	
main	The **main** advantage lies in continuous data acquisition.	Haupt-, hauptsächlich
mainly	Some methodological deficits, **mainly** the low number of patients, have to be named here.	hauptsächlich
largely	Current reports of laparoscopic cholecystectomy **largely** reflect the experience of early practitioners.	überwiegend, größtenteils
in large part	The high mortality rate associated with this disorder has not changed significantly over the past decades, **in large part** owing to delayed diagnosis.	zu einem großen Teil
for the most part	These published series represent, **for the most part**, the initial experience with laparoscopic cholecystectomy by each reporting institution. **For the most part**, image quality was very good.	zum größten Teil, größtenteils
predominantly	Soil microbiology **predominantly** deals with ...	vorwiegend

Mengenangaben (weiterführend)

vast	The **vast** majority of ischemic strokes results from ...	groß, überwiegend
considerable	There are **considerable** variations between different institutions.	beträchtlich
extensive	Surgeons who learn the new procedure in the future will no longer have **extensive** experience with traditional techniques.	weitreichend
extent (of)	The **extent** to which guanidine salts act as antiviral agents has yet to be determined. The **extent of** climatic changes related to the continued use of fossil fuels is difficult to measure.	Ausmaß (von), Tragweite
degree	The **degree** to which image quality is enhanced, strongly depends on patient positioning.	Grad
to vary from ... to ...	Contemporary rates of bile duct injury during open cholecystectomy **vary from** 0% **to** 0.4% and are often cited at 0.1% to 0.25%.	von ... bis ... variieren, von ... bis ... schwanken
to range from ... to ...	The reported death rates **range from** 0% **to** 0.4%.	von ... bis ... reichen
variability	We note that there is considerable intersubject **variability** in ...	Vielfalt, Variabilität

Mengenangaben (weiterführend)

variation	There is significant **variation** in ...	Variabilität, Schwankungsbreite

> **Info:** Im Zusammenhang mit statistischen Daten sollte statt **variability** bevorzugt **variation** verwendet werden, jedoch werden beide Begriffe häufig synonym gebraucht.

to exceed	The safety of this method remains doubtful, with reintervention rates **exceeding** 40%.	übersteigen, übertreffen
	These results have **exceeded** our initial expectations by far.	
to minimize	We can, however, **minimize** artefacts by careful positioning of the artefact-causing structures.	minimieren
to maximize	Efficiency can be **maximized** by using ...	maximieren

D 15. How to integrate aspects of time / Zeitliche Angaben

Basisvokabular

past	vergangen *auch:* Vergangenheit
previous	vorhergehend, früher
recent	kürzlich
so far	bis jetzt
to date	bislang, bisher
present	gegenwärtig; *bei Daten auch:* vorliegend
current	gegenwärtig, aktuell
future	zukünftig *auch:* Zukunft
initial	anfänglich
final	abschließend, endgültig

Aufbauvokabular und Satzbeispiele

past	These issues were intensively discussed in the **past**.	vergangen *auch:* Vergangenheit
previous	**Previous** studies have reported comparable results.	vorhergehend, früher
recent	In a **recent** study, Smith et al. conclude that ...	kürzlich

Zeitliche Angaben

so far	**So far**, no comparable technique has been implemented. No comparable technique has been implemented **so far**.	bis jetzt
thus far	More than half of the patients should have shown signs of recovery at this stage but they haven't done so, **thus far**.	bis jetzt *Info: stilistisch höher anzusetzen als* **so far**. *Gebräuchlich zur Vermeidung eines doppelten* **so**.
to date	This the largest series **to date** ... We have not identified, **to date**, any late bile duct complications.	bislang, bisher
present	The **present** data suggest that ...	gegenwärtig; *bei Daten auch:* vorliegend
current	**Current** reports of laparoscopic sigmoidectomy largely reflect the experience of early practitioners.	gegenwärtig, aktuell
future	Whether the use of combined PET/CT-systems is cost-effective will be subject to **future** investigation.	zukünftig *auch:* Zukunft
initial	These results reflect the **initial** experience of each surgeon. Obesity was **initially** considered a contraindication to the endoscopic procedure.	anfänglich
final	The **final** version includes several important guidelines.	abschließend, endgültig

D 16. How to analyse details / Detailanalyse

Basisvokabular

to go into detail	ins Detail gehen
in detail	detailliert
to detail (s.th.)	etw. genauer/detailliert erläutern
detailed	detailliert
thorough	gründlich, tiefschürfend
meticulous	(äußerst) sorgfältig, (äußerst) gründlich
extensive	umfassend, weitreichend
exhaustive	erschöpfend, eingehend
intensive	intensiv
to take a closer look at s.th.	etw. genauer betrachten

Aufbauvokabular und Satzbeispiele

to go into detail	We don't have to **go into detail** to recognize that ...	ins Detail gehen
in detail	We have researched the progress of this disease **in** great **detail**.	detailliert
to detail (s.th.)	Table 1 **details** the range of the lateral atlanto-dental interval asymmetry.	etw. genauer erläutern, etw. detailliert erläutern
detailed	Smith et al. have given a **detailed** description of the underlying biochemical interactions.	detailliert

Detailanalyse

thorough	A **thorough** analysis of ... has yielded the subsequent results.	gründlich, tiefschürfend
meticulous	A **meticulous** analysis of ...	(äußerst) sorgfältig, (äußerst) gründlich
extensive	Here we conduct an **extensive** investigation of ...	umfassend, weitreichend
exhaustive	An **exhaustive** description of ...	erschöpfend, eingehend
intensive	Despite **intensive** research, the architecture of ... remains poorly understood.	intensiv
to take a closer look at s.th.	**Taking a closer look at** acetogenesis, we have to admit that ...	etw. genauer betrachten
a closer examination	**A closer examination** of 27 major bile duct injuries in this report revealed that 67% occurred within each individual surgeon's first 25 cases.	eine eingehende Untersuchung
to scrutinize	The complex interaction between ... and ... was **scrutinized** by Smith et al.	(genauestens) erforschen, (genauestens) untersuchen
to focus on s.th.	In our analysis, we **focused/focussed on** those patients who ...	sich besonders mit etw. befassen, sich auf etw. konzentrieren
		Info: Beide Schreibweisen sind gebräuchlich.
a minute detail	But that is nothing more than **a minute detail**.	ein unbedeutendes Detail, ein winziges Detail

D 17. How to point out problems and limitations / Probleme und Limitierungen der Studie

Info: Da die nachfolgenden Vokabeln für dieses Kapitel von gleichrangiger Bedeutung sind, wird auf eine Unterteilung in Basis- und Aufbauvokabular verzichtet.

limitation	This study had (certain) **limitations**.	Limitierung
	Several **limitations** should be pointed out in the current study.	
	Small sample size was the major **limitation** of this study.	
	This study is subject to the inherent **limitations** of any survey-based data.	
to encounter limitations	While these advantages are important, some **limitations were encountered**.	an Grenzen stoßen
to be limited (by)	Our study, like others, **was limited by** the inability to prove with certainty the metastatic nature of all lesions detected with positron emission tomography.	limitiert sein (durch)
problem	One **problem** inherent in a study of this kind is the definition of surgical complications.	Problem
to face a problem	When we set out to investigate the phenomenon of ..., we had to **face** three major **problems**.	einem Problem gegenüberstehen
to be faced with a problem	In adopting the whole-body scan approach, we **were faced with the problem** of the upper extremities.	mit einem Problem konfrontiert werden

E Summary / Zusammenfassung

Basisvokabular

in summary	zusammengefasst, alles in allem
to sum up	zusammenfassen, *hier:* zusammenfassend
to summarize	zusammenfassen
finally	abschließend, schließlich
overall	insgesamt
in conclusion	am Ende, schließlich
to conclude	*hier:* abschließend (*auch:* schlussfolgern)

Aufbauvokabular und Satzbeispiele

in summary	**In summary**, our results clearly showed that …	zusammengefasst, alles in allem
to sum up	**To sum up**, digital radiography has successfully replaced conventional imaging systems in our institution.	zusammenfassen, *hier:* zusammenfassend
summing up	**Summing up**, the results of this large national survey demonstrate that laparoscopic cholecystectomy is essentially a safe procedure with low morbidity and mortality rates.	zusammenfassend
to summarize	Our results can be **summarized** as follows: …	zusammenfassen

Zusammenfassung

finally	**Finally**, the results of this study lead us to the conclusion that ...	abschließend, schließlich
overall	**Overall**, this investigation showed that ...	insgesamt
in conclusion	**In conclusion**, we may postulate that ...	am Ende, schließlich
to conclude	**To conclude**, we strongly recommend interventional procedures for patients who ...	*hier:* abschließend (*auch:* schlussfolgern)
in a final analysis	**In a final analysis**, these results demonstrate ...	abschließend betrachtet
on the whole	**On the whole**, early surgery in case of suspected small bowel ischemia has lead to ...	alles in allem

F Acknowledgements / Danksagungen

Basisvokabular

acknowledgement (BE) acknowledgment (AE)	Anerkennung; *im Plural:* Danksagung
help	Hilfe
assistance	Assistenz, Unterstützung, Beistand
advice	Rat
to thank	danken
to be grateful to	dankbar sein
to acknowledge	würdigen, anerkennen
to fund	(finanziell) unterstützen, bezuschussen
support	Unterstützung
to support	unterstützen

Aufbauvokabular und Satzbeispiele

to thank help	The authors **thank** ... for their **help** on cluster analysis.	danken Hilfe
support	The authors **thank** the staff of the Cyclotron Unit for their interest and **support**, especially the radiographers for their invaluable technical assistance.	Unterstützung

Danksagungen

assistance	We **thank** Ralph Stanton for his excellent technical **assistance**.	Assistenz, Unterstützung, Beistand
	We **thank** Jill Herrera for her administrative **assistance**.	
to be grateful to advice	The authors **are grateful to** ... for **advice** and **support** in performing these studies.	dankbar sein Rat
to acknowledge	The authors gratefully **acknowledge** Petra Huber and ... for their **help** with the bone scintigraphy quantifications; Matthias Plevic for his **support** with data collection; and all involved physicians, nurses, technicians, and members of the Department of Nuclear Medicine.	würdigen, anerkennen
	The **assistance** of the Nuclear Medicine staff in acquiring data is gratefully **acknowledged**.	
to address thanks to s.o.	The authors **address** special **thanks to** ...	jmdm. danken, Dank an jmdn. richten
to extend thanks to s.o.	We wish to **extend** special **thanks to** ...	jmdm. danken, Dank an jmdn. richten
to express gratitude to s.o.	We also **express gratitude to** ...	jmdm. gegenüber Dankbarkeit zum Ausdruck bringen
to show appreciation to s.o.	The authors also **show appreciation to** the doctors in the Department of Cardiology (Sunhill Medical Centre).	jmdn. dankend erwähnen (*wörtlich:* Wertschätzung ausdrücken)
Thanks are due to s.o.	**Thanks are** also **due to** Ella Lindberg ...	Dank gebührt jmdm.

Danksagungen

to fund	This study was **funded** by ...	(finanziell) unterstützen, bezuschussen
	This study was **funded** in part by grants from the National Institute of ...	
	This research was **funded** by the European Commission Research Project ...	
to support	This research was **supported** in part by ...	unterstützen
	This work was **supported** by a grant from the University of ...	

II. Oral presentation / Vorträge

1. How to welcome and guide the audience – Begrüßung und Moderation

Words of welcome	Begrüßungsfloskeln
Ladies and gentlemen, welcome to the annual meeting of the European Association of ...	Meine Damen und Herren, willkommen zur Jahrestagung der Europäischen Gesellschaft für …
Welcome to the session on ...	Willkommen zur Session über ...
Good morning, ladies and gentlemen. I am pleased to announce the session on ...	Guten Morgen, meine Damen und Herren. Ich freue mich, Ihnen die Session über … ankündigen zu dürfen.
Good evening, ladies and gentlemen, we continue with the lecture on ...	Guten Abend, meine Damen und Herren, wir fahren fort mit dem Vortrag/der Vorlesung über …

Introducing the speakers	Vorstellen der Referenten
The first speaker I'd like to announce is ...	Der erste Vortragende, den ich ankündigen möchte, ist …
Now I'd like to introduce the second speaker.	Nun möchte ich Ihnen den zweiten Redner vorstellen.
I'd like Mr. Smith to take the floor.	Ich möchte gerne Herrn Smith das Wort erteilen.
I would like to call Mr. Smith to the podium.	Ich möchte gerne Herrn Smith zum Podium bitten.
It's a great pleasure for me to introduce Mr. Smith.	Es ist mir eine große Freude, Ihnen Herrn Smith vorstellen zu dürfen.

It is my great pleasure to introduce Ms. Taylor.	Ich freue mich, Ihnen Frau Taylor vorstellen zu dürfen.
I am very happy to welcome the next speaker, Ms. Taylor, who has managed to fill in for Mr. Smith at very short notice.	Ich bin sehr glücklich, die nächste Rednerin, Frau Taylor, willkommen zu heißen, die es geschafft hat, sehr kurzfristig für Herrn Smith einzuspringen.
We now finish up this morning session with the lecture of Ms. ...	Wir beenden die Vormittags-Session mit dem Vortrag/der Vorlesung von Frau ...
Mr. Smith, I believe you are the expert in this field.	Herr Smith, ich glaube, Sie sind der Experte auf diesem Gebiet.

Thanking the speakers / Dank an den Vortragenden

Thank you very much for this interesting lecture on ...	Vielen Dank für diesen interessanten Vortrag/diese interessante Vorlesung über ...
Thank you for this comprehensive overview.	Dankeschön für diesen umfassenden Überblick.
Thank you, Ms. Taylor, for your riveting contribution on the latest developments in ...	Frau Taylor, danke für Ihren fesselnden Beitrag über die jüngsten Entwicklungen auf dem Gebiet der ...
Dr. Smith really provided an excellent survey.	Dr. Smith hat wirklich einen exzellenten Überblick präsentiert.

2. Introduction – Einleitung

Polite opening	Eröffnungsfloskeln
Thank you, Mr. Chairman.	Danke, Herr Vorsitzender.
Thanks for having me here tonight.	Danke, dass ich heute Abend hier sein darf.
Thank you very much for inviting me.	Vielen Dank, dass Sie mich eingeladen haben.
It's a great pleasure for me to follow this invitation.	Es ist mir eine große Freude, dieser Einladung zu folgen.
I feel honoured to speak here today.	Es ist mir eine Ehre, heute hier zu sprechen.

Topic and aim of the lecture	Thema und Ziel des Vortrags
This lecture is about …	In diesem Vortrag/dieser Vorlesung geht es um …
This session is on …	Dieser Vortrag/diese Vorlesung/diese Session behandelt/befasst sich mit …
In this lecture, I'm going to report …	In diesem Vortrag/dieser Vorlesung werde ich … berichten.
In this lecture, I'm going to present the results of …	In diesem Vortrag/dieser Vorlesung werde ich die Ergebnisse von … vorstellen.
What I'm going to present is …	Was ich (Ihnen) vorstellen/zeigen möchte, ist …
My presentation mainly deals with …	Ich referiere im Wesentlichen über…

Einleitung

During the next few minutes, I'd like to ...	In den nächsten Minuten möchte ich ...
The aim of my lecture is ...	Das Ziel meines Vortrags ist ...
The objective is to ...	Ziel ist es, ...

Structure of the lecture / Gliederung des Vortrags

First of all, a word on ...	Zunächst einmal ein paar Worte über ...
Let's start/begin with ...	Lassen Sie uns mit ... beginnen.
To start with, I'll give you an overview of ...	Zu Beginn/Als Einstieg möchte ich Ihnen einen Überblick über ... geben.
To start, I want to show you ...	Zu Beginn/Als Einstieg möchte ich Ihnen ... zeigen.
I'd like to touch upon ...	Ich möchte kurz auf ... eingehen.
Our goals are first, to review the basic principles of ...	Unsere Ziele bestehen zunächst darin, die grundlegenden Prinzipien von ... näher zu betrachten.
Then I am/we are going to talk about ...	Dann/danach werde ich/werden wir über ... sprechen.
The topics we are going to talk about are ...	Die Themen, über die wir sprechen werden, sind ...
At last, I would like to ...	Zum Schluss würde ich gerne ...
We will finish with ...	Wir werden mit ... schließen.
And finally, we are taking a closer look at ...	Und am Ende beschäftigen wir uns näher mit ...

3. How to link up passages – Überleitungen

Moving on	Weiter gehts
That's it for the introduction. Now ...	Soviel zur Einleitung. Jetzt ...
Now let's take a look at ...	Lassen Sie uns nun ... betrachten.
Now we move on to ...	Wir kommen nun zu ... Wir machen weiter mit ...
That brings me to ...	Das führt mich zu ...
This is another ...	Das ist ein weiteres/weiterer/eine weitere …
Before we proceed, we must consider ...	Bevor wir fortfahren, müssen wir … bedenken.
Just a few comments I'd like to make before ...	Lassen Sie mich nur ein paar Anmerkungen machen, bevor …
I'd like to proceed with some examples for ...	Ich möchte mit einigen Beispielen für … fortfahren.
Now that I have shown you ..., we proceed with ...	Nachdem ich Ihnen jetzt ... gezeigt habe, fahren wir fort mit …

Changing the subject	Themawechsel
Let me broach another subject/problem/question.	Lassen Sie mich ein weiteres Thema/Problem/eine weitere Frage ansprechen.
I want to take a moment to talk about ...	Ich möchte kurz auf ... eingehen.
Now I want to take a few minutes to talk about ...	Nun möchte ich ein paar Minuten auf … verwenden.

Überleitungen

I want to spend a minute or two on ...	Ich möchte ein, zwei Minuten über ... reden.
Just a word or two about ...	Nur ein, zwei Sätze zu ...
Another point to be mentioned in any discussion of this problem/issue, is ...	Was in jeglicher Diskussion dieses Problems/dieses Themas erwähnt werden muss, ist folgender Punkt ...
Now ...	*Universell verwendbare Überleitungsfüllsel, ohne Sinn tragende Übersetzung, an die sich jegliche Äußerung anschließen kann.*
So ...	

Moving back / Nochmal zurück

But back to ...	Doch zurück zu ...
Now we come back to ...	Wir kommen nun zurück zu ...
Let's go back to my introductory remarks on ...	Lassen Sie uns (kurz) auf meine einführenden Bemerkungen zurückkommen.
I'd like to return to what I said earlier on.	Ich würde gerne noch einmal auf das zurückkommen, was ich vorher gesagt habe.

End in sight / Zum Schluss kommen

Finally, I want to talk about ...	Zum Schluss möchte ich (noch) über ... sprechen.
We are going to move on to our penultimate/last topic.	Wir kommen nun zu unserem vorletzten/letzten Thema.
For the rest of the time, let me address ...	Lassen Sie mich in der verbleibenden Zeit ... ansprechen.

Überleitungen

Before finishing, I want to show you ...	Bevor ich zum Ende komme, möchte ich Ihnen ... zeigen.
My presentation is drawing to its end.	Ich bin gleich mit meinem Vortrag fertig.
We are almost finished.	Wir sind fast fertig.
If you will bear with me, I won't be keeping you long.	Wenn Sie mir noch kurz Gehör schenken wollen; ich werde nicht recht viel länger referieren.
Let's begin the discussion with ...	Beginnen wir die Diskussion mit ...

4. Slides, transparencies and graphics – Dias, Folien und grafische Elemente

Slide projection	**Diaprojektion**
Could I have the first slide, please?	Könnte ich bitte das erste Dia haben?
First slide, please.	Das erste Dia bitte.
Next slide, please.	Nächstes Dia bitte.
We have just skipped a slide there.	Wir haben ein Dia übersprungen.
Could you go back one slide, please?	Könnten Sie bitte ein Dia zurückgehen?
Back one more, please.	Noch eins (zurück), bitte.
Could I have the one before, please?	Könnte ich das vorherige (Dia) haben, bitte?
Could we go back to the very first slide again, please?	Könnten wir bitte das allererste Dia noch mal haben?

What you see	**Was man sieht**
The first slide shows you ...	Das erste Dia zeigt Ihnen ...
The second/next slide shows you ...	Das zweite/nächste Dia zeigt Ihnen ...
On the next slide you can see ...	Auf dem nächsten Dia können Sie ... sehen.
Here you can see ...	Hier sehen Sie ...
What you can also see is ...	Was Sie auch sehen können, ist ...

Dias, Folien und grafische Elemente

We are looking at …	Wir schauen auf …
	Wir sehen hier …
What we're looking at here is …	Was wir hier sehen, ist…
These images show …	Diese Bilder/Abbildungen zeigen …
The diagram on the right demonstrates …	Das rechte Diagramm zeigt/demonstriert …
The next transparency highlights …	Die nächste Folie beleuchtet … näher.
This slide looks very busy.	Dieses Dia sieht ziemlich überfrachtet/unübersichtlich aus.
This number should read 4.0 instead of 40%.	Das soll 4,0 statt 40 % heißen.

Guiding the audience	**Aufmerksamkeit lenken**
Let's take a look at …	Werfen wir einen Blick auf …
	Sehen wir uns … an.
I want to draw your attention to …	Ich möchte ihre Aufmerksamkeit gerne auf … lenken.
May I draw your attention to …	Darf ich Ihre Aufmerksamkeit auf … lenken.
I call your attention to …	Richten Sie Ihre Aufmerksamkeit auf …
Please pay attention to …	Bitte richten Sie Ihre Aufmerksamkeit auf …
I would like you to pay special attention to …	Beachten Sie bitte vor allem …

Dias, Folien und grafische Elemente

(Please) Note that …	Beachten Sie (bitte), dass …
Notice that …	Nehmen Sie zur Kenntnis, dass …
You ought to focus on …	Sie sollten Ihr Augenmerk auf … richten.
at the top/bottom	oben/unten
on the right/left	rechts/links
in the middle/centre	in der Mitte
The upper part of the diagram shows …	Der obere Teil des Diagramms zeigt …
Please look at the lower right-hand corner of the slide.	Bitte betrachten Sie die rechte untere Ecke des Dias.

Giving examples — Beispiele anführen

Here is an example for …	Hier ist ein Beispiel für …
Let me show you one example for …	Lassen Sie mich Ihnen ein Beispiel für … zeigen.
I have got another example.	Ich habe ein weiteres Beispiel.
Yet another example for … is …	Und noch ein weiteres Beispiel für … ist …
To illustrate that point I'd like to show you…	Um dies zu veranschaulichen, möchte ich Ihnen … zeigen.

Technical problems — Verhalten bei technischen Problemen

I believe there is something wrong with the microphone/the mike.	Ich glaube, irgendetwas stimmt nicht mit dem Mikrophon/Mikro.

Dias, Folien und grafische Elemente

Can you all hear me without the microphone/the mike?	Kann mich jeder hören ohne Mikrophon/Mikro?
What's wrong with this pointer?	Was stimmt mit diesem Pointer nicht?
I'm afraid this pointer is not working (properly).	Ich fürchte, dieser Pointer funktioniert nicht (richtig).
This is not the slide I wanted.	Das ist nicht das Dia, das ich wollte.
Looks like we are having some technical problem.	Sieht aus, als hätten wir hier ein technisches Problem.
That's not part of the presentation.	Das gehört nicht zum Vortrag.
What's going on?	Was ist da los?

Universell verwendbare Äußerungen bei unvorhergesehenen Problemen.

5. How to emphasize – Hervorhebungen

I want to emphasize (to you) that ...	Ich möchte (Ihnen gegenüber) betonen, dass …
We have to emphasize that ...	Man muss betonen, dass ...
I'd like to put the emphasis on ...	Ich möchte den Schwerpunkt/die Betonung auf … legen.
I'd like to stress again that ...	Ich möchte noch einmal betonen, dass …
I'd like to point out that …	Ich möchte darauf hinweisen, dass …
What is important is ...	Was wichtig ist, ist ...
What is most important is that ...	Was am wichtigsten ist, ist …
That's a very important finding.	Das ist eine sehr wichtige Beobachtung/Feststellung.
There is another important feature that I want you to be aware of: ...	Ich möchte, dass Sie sich noch einen anderen wichtigen Aspekt vor Augen führen: …
What matters (most) is (the fact) that ...	Worauf es (am meisten) ankommt, ist (die Tatsache), dass …
One of the issues to underscore is ...	Eines der Themen, die man unterstreichen muss, ist …
One of the key issues is ...	Eines der entscheidenden Themen ist …
This is what I want to say!	Darum geht es mir!
	Das ist es, worauf ich hinaus will!

6. Summary / Closing Remarks – Zusammenfassung / Schlusswort

Summary	Zusammenfassung
All in all, …	Alles in allem …
In one word, …	Mit einem Wort …/Kurzum …
Summing up, ...	Zusammenfassend …
To sum up, ...	Zusammenfassend …
In summary, what I have tried to show you is ...	Um zusammenzufassen: Was ich versucht habe, Ihnen zu zeigen …
Let me summarize the aforementioned results in one simple phrase.	Lassen Sie mich die bisher genannten Ergebnisse auf eine Formel bringen/in einem einfachen Satz zusammenfassen.
Taking everything into account, ...	Wenn man all das/alles berücksichtigt, …
Taking everything into consideration, ...	Wenn man all das/alles berücksichtigt, …

Closing remarks	Schlusswort
To conclude, I would like to ...	Abschließend würde ich gerne …
In conclusion we may say that ...	Abschließend kann man sagen, dass …
Let me conclude ...	Lassen Sie mich abschließen ...
With those remarks, I'd like to conclude ...	Mit diesen Anmerkungen möchte ich (ab)schließen …

Take-Home-Message	Kernaussage
So what the study has shown is ...	Was die Studie also gezeigt hat, ist ...
What I want you to take home is ...	Was Sie mit nach Hause nehmen sollen, ist ...
The take home message (here) is ...	Die „Take-Home-Message" ist ...
The gist of this study is as follows: ...	Das Wesentliche dieser Studie lautet wie folgt: ...
The bottom line of this survey is ...	Die Kernaussage dieser Studie lautet ...

Thanking the audience	Dank an Publikum
Thank you.	Dankeschön.
Thank you for your attention.	Danke für Ihre Aufmerksamkeit.
Thanks for your attention.	Danke für Ihre Aufmerksamkeit.
Thank you for your time, ladies and gentlemen.	Ich danke Ihnen (für Ihre Zeit), meine Damen und Herren.

7. How to invite the audience to ask questions – Aufforderung zu Fragen

At the beginning of the lecture	Am Anfang des Vortrags
If you have any questions, I'll be glad to answer them at the end of my presentation.	Sollten Sie Fragen haben, so werde ich diese gerne am Ende meines Vortrages beantworten.
Please stop me any time you have a question.	Bitte stoppen Sie mich jederzeit, wenn Sie eine Frage haben.
I don't mind being interrupted if there is any question.	Sie dürfen mich gerne unterbrechen, wenn es Fragen gibt.
If there is any question to ask, please feel free to do so.	Wenn es irgendeine Frage gibt, fragen Sie einfach.
If you have any questions, please feel free to interrupt.	Sollte es irgendwelche Fragen geben, so fragen Sie einfach.

During the lecture	Während des Vortrags
Does anybody have any questions right now?	Gibt es dazu momentan (irgendwelche) Fragen?
Before we continue, are there any questions or comments on ...?	Bevor wir fortfahren, gibt es (irgendwelche) Fragen oder Kommentare zu …?
I'd like to move on (to ...) unless there are any questions.	Ich würde dann gerne (mit …) fortfahren, es sei denn, es gibt irgendwelche Fragen.
If there are no further questions I'd like to proceed to the next section of my presentation.	Wenn Sie keine weiteren Fragen haben, dann würde ich gerne mit dem nächsten Abschnitt meines Vortrages fortfahren.

Aufforderung zu Fragen

Has anyone anything further they wish to add before we move on to the next issue?	Hat jemand noch etwas, das er vorbringen möchte, bevor wir zum nächsten Thema/Punkt übergehen?

> *Info:* Äußerst gebräuchliche Universalkonstruktion um Personen beiderlei Geschlechts anzusprechen; vgl.: Everybody gets what they deserve.

Fire away!	Schießen Sie los!
Go ahead!	Nur zu!

> *Info:* Informell, aber durchaus gebräuchlich, als Reaktion auf eine Anfrage aus dem Publikum i.S.v.: Would you mind if I asked a few questions right now?

At the end of the lecture / Am Ende des Vortrags

Have you got any questions?	Haben Sie Fragen? *(BE)*
Do you have any questions?	Haben Sie Fragen? *(AE; verdrängt zunehmend die BE-Variante)*
Have you any questions?	Haben Sie Fragen? *(BE/AE; sehr förmlich)*
I am happy to take any question now.	Ich beantworte jetzt gerne jede Frage.
I'll be happy to answer any question.	Ich werde gerne jede Frage beantworten.
Are there any other questions?	Gibt es (noch) andere Fragen?
Are there any more questions?	Gibt es noch Fragen?
Any further questions on this?	(Gibt es) weitere Fragen hierzu?
Any further points before we bring this meeting/session to an end?	(Gibt es) weitere Punkte bevor wir die Sitzung schließen?

8. How to answer and retort – Antwort auf Fragen, Anmerkungen und Einwände

Universals	Neutrale Antwortfloskeln
Thanks for bringing this up.	Danke, dass Sie das sagen.
Thank you for this interesting question.	Danke für diese interessante Frage.
Thank you for your contribution.	Danke für Ihren Beitrag.
You have just mentioned something very important.	Sie sprechen da etwas sehr Wichtiges an.
You have just raised a very important point.	Sie haben soeben einen sehr wichtigen Punkt angesprochen.
Your question leads us straight back to the subject.	Ihre Frage führt uns unmittelbar zum Thema zurück.

Agreement	Zustimmung
That's true.	Das ist wahr.
That's right.	Das ist richtig.
You are exactly right!	Sie haben genau Recht!
You are absolutely right in saying that …	Sie haben absolut Recht, wenn Sie sagen, dass …
Absolutely!	Absolut (richtig)!
Certainly!	Mit Sicherheit!
Definitely!	Ganz genau!
Exactly!	Exakt!
Spot on!	Den Nagel auf den Kopf getroffen! *(sinngemäß)*

Antwort auf Fragen ...

I agree with you.	Ich stimme Ihnen zu.
I agree with Dr. Smith on that point.	Ich stimme Dr. Smith in dieser Sache zu.
I quite agree with Dr. Smith.	Ich stimme Dr. Smith völlig zu.
	(Anm.: British understatement i.S.v. That was quite good = Das war gar nicht schlecht/Das war sehr gut)
I fully agree with Dr. Smith.	Ich stimme Dr. Smith voll und ganz zu.
I think we are all agreed on that.	Ich denke, in diesem Punkt stimmen wir alle überein.
I concur with my colleague.	Ich stimme mit meinem Kollegen überein.
I concur on that point.	Ich gehe in diesem Punkt konform.
I am entirely of your opinion.	Ich bin völlig Ihrer Meinung.
That's a very good point!	Gut, dass Sie das sagen…
	Sehr guter Hinweis!
This is beyond question.	Das steht außer Frage.
I must admit that ...	Ich muss zugeben, dass …

Restricted agreement — Eingeschränkte Zustimmung

You are right, in a way.	In gewisser Hinsicht haben Sie Recht.
You are partially right.	Zum Teil haben Sie Recht.
You are not completely wrong, but ...	Sie haben nicht ganz Unrecht, aber …
It depends.	Kommt darauf an.

Antwort auf Fragen ...

Although it must be admitted that ..., there is no denying the fact that ...	Zugegebenermaßen ..., dennoch lässt sich nicht abstreiten, dass ...
Concerning method A, you are right.	Was Methode A anbelangt, haben Sie Recht.

Disagreement / Widerspruch

You misunderstood me.	Sie haben mich missverstanden.
Perhaps I haven't made myself clear. What I'm trying to say is ...	Vielleicht habe ich mich unklar ausgedrückt. Was ich versuche, zu sagen, ist...
At the risk of repeating myself, (but) ...	Auf die Gefahr hin, mich zu wiederholen, (aber) ...
I would question this assertion.	Ich würde diese Behauptung in Frage stellen.
I don't agree with you.	Ich bin anderer Meinung.
I take a different view.	Ich sehe das anders.
This is definitely not the point!	Darum geht es hier überhaupt nicht!
This is simply wrong, since ...	Das ist schlichtweg falsch, da ...
By no means!	Keineswegs!
Far from it!	Weit gefehlt!
Your remarks are a little bit of the mark, I'm afraid.	Ich fürchte, mit Ihren Bemerkungen liegen Sie ein wenig daneben. (i.S.v. „Ihre Bemerkungen sind fast schon irrelevant")
With (all) due respect, Mr. Smith, ...	Bei allem Respekt/Ihre Meinung in Ehren, Herr Smith, ...

Antwort auf Fragen ...

Let me get this straight!	Um das ganz klar zu stellen ... Lassen Sie mich in aller Deutlichkeit sagen ...
It is my considered opinion that ...	Es ist meine fundierte Meinung, dass ...

Doubts and uncertainties / Zweifel und Unklarheiten

I'm not quite sure about ...	Ich bin mir da nicht so sicher.
That remains to be seen.	Das bleibt abzuwarten.
That has yet to be proven.	Das muss erst noch bewiesen werden.
This is still under discussion.	Das ist noch nicht geklärt.
We don't know this (for sure).	Das wissen wir nicht (mit Sicherheit).

If you have no answer / Wenn Sie keine Antwort wissen

I have no answer to your question at the moment.	Ich kann Ihre Frage im Moment nicht beantworten.
You have caught me off my guard!	Jetzt haben Sie mich (blank) erwischt!
I find myself on unfamiliar territory.	Auf diesem Gebiet bin ich etwas unbewandert.
Mr. Smith is a much better person to answer your question.	Herr Smith kann Ihre Frage weit besser beantworten.
This question cannot be answered in a nutshell.	Diese Frage lässt sich nicht mit einem Satz beantworten.

Antwort auf Fragen ...

Answering your question would be outside the scope of my presentation.	Die Antwort auf Ihre Frage würde den Rahmen meines Vortrages sprengen.
At the moment I don't have enough information at my disposal (to sufficiently answer your question).	Mir stehen momentan nicht genügend Informationen zur Verfügung (um Ihre Frage ausreichend zu beantworten).
We should leave that for later.	Das sollten wir uns für später aufheben.
I would like to put this question off till later.	Diese Frage würde ich gerne auf später verschieben.
I suggest we defer this matter until ...	Ich schlage vor, wir vertagen/verschieben diese Angelegenheit bis ...
I'm sorry, but I fail to see your point.	Es tut mir leid, ich weiß nicht, worauf Sie hinaus wollen.

Multiple questions — Mehr als eine Frage

The answer to your first question is ...	Die Antwort auf Ihre erste Frage lautet ...
Let me answer your last question first.	Lassen Sie mich Ihre letzte Frage zuerst beantworten.
Now for your next question.	Nun zu Ihrer nächsten Frage.
Could you please repeat your second question?	Könnten Sie Ihre zweite Frage bitte noch einmal wiederholen?

9. How to ask and comment – Fragen und Kommentare anbringen

Direct questions	Direkte Fragen
I have a question.	Ich habe eine Frage.
I've got a question.	Ich habe eine Frage. *(BE)*
May I ask (you) a question?	Darf ich (Ihnen) eine Frage stellen?
I would like to ask you whether ...	Ich würde Sie gerne fragen, ob ...
I would like to know if ...	Ich würde gerne wissen, ob ... Mich würde interessieren, ob ...
I am wondering how you ...	Ich frage mich, wie Sie ...
It would be interesting to know ...	Es wäre interessant zu wissen, ...
Two questions still remain.	Zwei Fragen sind noch offen.
There's a question I'd like to ask.	Ich möchte eine Frage stellen. *(betont)*
I do have another question!	Ich habe da schon noch eine Frage! *(betont; diese Form ist angebracht, wenn der Redner davon ausgeht, dass es keine Fragen (mehr) gibt)*
... how shall I put it? ... Let me rephrase my question.	... wie soll ich sagen? ... Lassen Sie es mich anders formulieren.
I'm afraid I didn't quite follow.	Ich habe Ihnen leider nicht ganz folgen können.

Fragen und Kommentare ...

Requests	Aufforderungen
Could you please explain once more how ...	Könnten Sie bitte noch einmal erklären, wie ...
Would you mind giving another example for ...?	Könnten sie ein weiteres Beispiel für ... anführen?
Could you expand on that?	Könnten Sie das noch weiter ausführen?
Would you like to elaborate on that?	Würden Sie darauf noch näher eingehen?
Maybe you could show the previous slide again. I think there is some contradiction in the figures.	Vielleicht könnten Sie das letzte/vorherige Dia noch einmal zeigen. Ich glaube, dass sich die Zahlen widersprechen.
At the risk of sounding offensive, I should very much appreciate if you would answer my question.	Ich möchte Ihnen nicht zu nahe treten, aber ich würde es sehr begrüßen, wenn Sie meine Frage (endlich) beantworten würden.
Please correct me if I'm wrong.	Korrigieren Sie mich bitte, falls ich hier falsch liege.

Comment preceding question	Frage mit einleitendem Kommentar
This was indeed a very interesting presentation. However, there is one thing I'd like you to explain.	Das war in der Tat eine sehr interessante Präsentation. Dennoch würde ich Sie bitten, einen Punkt zu erläutern.
I found your lecture quite accomplished. Yet, it has raised a few questions.	Ich fand Ihren Vortrag/Ihre Vorlesung sehr gelungen. Dennoch wirft er/sie einige Fragen auf.

At the beginning of your presentation, you mentioned ... Could you please provide more information on how this would fit into Dr. Wagner's model?	Zu Beginn Ihrer Präsentation erwähnten Sie ... Können Sie uns mehr darüber sagen, wie dies mit Dr. Wagners Modell in Einklang zu bringen ist? *(sinngemäß)*

Interrupting with a question / Den Vortragenden mit einer Frage unterbrechen

Excuse me, may I interrupt you?	Verzeihung, darf ich Sie unterbrechen?
Sorry for interrupting you. Could you perhaps ...	Entschuldigen Sie, dass ich Sie unterbreche. Könnten Sie vielleicht ...
Sorry to break in/to cut in.	Es tut mir leid, dass ich Sie unterbreche.
May I come in at this point?	Darf ich Sie hier kurz unterbrechen?
If you permit, I'd like to mention that ...	Wenn Sie gestatten, möchte ich erwähnen, dass ...
With your permission, Sir, I'd like to add some information on ...	Wenn Sie gestatten, möchte ich einige Informationen über ... anfügen.
Excuse me Madam/Sir! Before you proceed, I would like to ask ...	Entschuldigen Sie bitte! Bevor Sie fortfahren, würde ich gerne noch fragen ...
Excuse me, but before we move on to the next item, I'd like to ...	Entschuldigen Sie, aber bevor wir zum nächsten Punkt/Thema kommen, möchte ich gerne ...
I do apologize, but this is simply wrong!	Entschuldigen Sie bitte, aber das ist schlichtweg falsch!

Fragen und Kommentare …

Comments	Kommentare
I would like to say/add something.	Ich würde gerne etwas vorbringen/ergänzen.
There is something I would like to say.	Ich würde gerne etwas vorbringen. *(betont)*
I would like to comment on …	Ich würde gerne zu … etwas sagen.
I'd like to come back to what you've said about …	Ich würde gerne auf Ihre Ausführungen über … zurückkommen.
I'd like to return to what Ms. Taylor has just said.	Ich würde gerne auf das zurückkommen, was Frau Taylor soeben gesagt hat.
Let me take up again what Mr. Smith has mentioned.	Lassen Sie mich nochmals aufgreifen, was Herr Smith gesagt hat.
Coming back to what you said earlier on, I would ask you to go more into detail.	Um auf das zurück zu kommen, was Sie zuvor gesagt haben, möchte ich Sie bitten, mehr ins Detail zu gehen.
You gave a very detailed overview of … Yet, there are some crucial aspects that need mentioning/need to be mentioned.	Sie haben (uns) einen sehr detaillierten Überblick über … gegeben. Es sind jedoch noch ein paar entscheidende Punkte zu erwähnen.
Listening to you and the previous speakers, I get the impression that …	Wenn ich Ihnen und den Vorrednern zuhöre, habe ich den Eindruck, dass …
Am I right?	Sehe ich das richtig?
Is this correct?	Stimmt das so?
Please correct me if I'm wrong.	Verbessern Sie mich bitte, wenn ich da falsch liege.

Appendix 1 — How to submit / Manuskripteinsendung

Grundsätzlich haben Sie zwei Möglichkeiten der Manuskripteinsendung: Sie können das Manuskript als Papierausdruck oder aber über die entsprechende Internetseite der wissenschaftlichen Zeitschrift online versenden.
Letzteres wird heutzutage von den meisten Zeitschriften bevorzugt. Der Autor muss sich in der Regel mit Benutzername *(username)* und Passwort *(password)* registrieren. Hierbei wird man Schritt für Schritt durch eine Reihe von Eingabefenstern geführt.
Bei vielen Verlagen ist mit der Registrierung auch eine Abfrage des Manuskriptstatus möglich; häufig erhält der Benutzer Zugriff auf Online-Datenbanken und Kurzfassungen bereits veröffentlichter Artikel.
Details zur Manuskriptvorbereitung und -einsendung sind bei allen gängigen Magazinen auf der Internetseite abrufbar (die Rubriken heißen meist *For authors, Author guidelines, Preparing your manuscript, Submission guidelines, How to submit, Manuscript submission, Submitting your manuscript* etc.). Manche Zeitschriften akzeptieren keine unaufgefordert eingesandten Manuskripte *(no unsolicited material)*.
Verschiedene Redaktionen haben oft sehr unterschiedliche formale Anforderungen an ein Manuskript, weshalb Sie in jedem Falle die spezifischen Anweisungen und Anforderungen für Ihre Manuskripteinsendung beachten müssen. Die nachfolgend aufgeführten Punkte stellen lediglich eine kurze Zusammenfassung wichtiger Kriterien dar.

Im Allgemeinen gilt, dass das Manuskript von Ihnen verfasst sein muss, bisher unveröffentlicht *(previously unpublished)* ist und nicht gleichzeitig an andere Zeitschriften gesandt wurde *(not under consideration for publication elsewhere; no simultaneous submissions)*.

Für die Manuskripteinsendung sollten Sie folgende Dinge parat halten:

1. Eine knappe Zusammenfassung Ihres Artikels *(synopsis; abstract)*.
2. Den Artikel im geforderten Format.
3. Ein Begleitschreiben *(cover letter)*.
4. Alle weiteren von der Redaktion geforderten Angaben zu *authorship responsibility, copyright transfer, financial disclosure* etc.
   (Hier sei auf die *submission guidelines* der Zeitschriften verwiesen.)

Zu 1.:

In den *submission guidelines* der Redaktionen finden Sie Angaben zu Inhalten und Umfang des *abstract*. Üblicherweise wird hier eine kurze Beschreibung Ihrer Arbeit sowie der wichtigsten Thesen und Schlussfolgerungen gefordert.

Manuskripteinsendung

Zu 2.:

Achten Sie auf Vorgaben zum Format: Papierausdrucke *(hard copy)* sollen oft im jeweiligen Landesformat, also z.b. *US letter format* anstatt DIN A 4 eingesandt werden. Für elektronische Einsendungen *(electronic submission)* sind nur bestimmte Dateiformate erlaubt (z.B. WORD .doc, .rtf oder .pdf).
Auch hier gelten häufig Beschränkungen hinsichtlich Umfang bzw. Wortzahl.

Zur Gliederung eines Manuskripts gibt es sehr unterschiedliche Vorgaben. Die folgende Variante stellt eine elementare Struktur für ein wissenschaftliches Manuskript dar. Diese liegt auch dem Aufbau dieses Buches zugrunde.

1. Introduction
2. Materials and methods
3. Results
4. Discussion/Conclusion
5. Acknowledgements
6. References

Je nach Art der Arbeit und redaktionellen Vorgaben sind hier natürlich zahlreiche Variationen möglich.
Sehr oft wird der Abschnitt *Materials and methods* als *Supplementary Information* gar nicht mehr in der Printversion publiziert, sondern nur im Internetauftritt der Zeitschrift.

Zu 3.:

Im *cover letter* sollten folgende Punkte enthalten sein:

- Titel des Manuskripts *(manuscript title, title of the paper)*
- Hauptaussage der Arbeit *(statement of the main point)*

Optional sind an dieser Stelle auch noch weitere Aspekte zu berücksichtigen (je nach *submission guidelines*):

- Manuskriptumfang/Wortzahl *(word count)*
- Namentlicher Vorschlag von Personen, die das Manuskript begutachten sollten *(reviewer)*
- Art der Publikation (*type of manuscript*; z.B. *original article, review, case report* etc.)
- Erwähnung weiterer Publikationen oder Vorträge, die in Bezug zur aktuellen Arbeit stehen

Einen Sonderfall stellt der *cover letter* für ein überarbeitetes *(revised)* Manuskript dar. Neben einer Zusammenfassung der vorgenommenen Änderungen am Manuskript sollte hier auf die Empfehlungen der *reviewer* explizit und Punkt für Punkt eingegangen werden.

Nachstehend finden Sie Musteranschreiben, die Ihnen eine Formulierungshilfe für Ihren individuellen *cover letter* bieten. Dabei wird auch auf Besonderheiten für den britischen und amerikanischen Sprachraum eingegangen.

Musteranschreiben für britische Fachzeitschrift

Musterstraße 1
12345 Musterhausen
Germany
e-mail: peter.muster@abc.de

Professor M.C. Smith, MD
Editor of JOURNAL NAME
17 Lake Road
Leeds
GW6 2AH
United Kingdom

17 May 2006

Dear Professor Smith[1]

Please find enclosed our manuscript *"Development of gallstone surgery in Germany 1991–2003: Results of a multicentre survey"*.
This retrospective analysis of 45,500 cholecystectomies describes the changes in diagnostic and therapeutic strategies following the introduction of laparoscopic cholecystectomy. Our work investigates the surgical and non-surgical complication rates, reintervention rates and mortality rates of conventional vs. laparoscopic cholecystectomy with special focus on treatment standards in choledocholithiasis. Our data confirm the outstanding role of the minimally-invasive surgical technique and reveal a clear trend towards endoscopic treatment of bile duct stones.
We believe this manuscript to be of interest to many readers of JOURNAL NAME and hope it is suitable for publication.

Yours sincerely[2]

Peter Muster, MD

---

[1] Nach der Anrede steht im BE kein Satzzeichen; allerdings kann ein Komma gesetzt werden. Ist die betreffende Person namentlich bekannt, so setzen Sie z. B. *Dear Professor Smith* und schließen mit *Yours sincerely*. Titel und Anredeformeln *(MD, Ms, Mr, Dr)* werden i.d.R. ohne Abkürzungspunkte angeführt. Sollten Sie keinen namentlichen Adressaten haben, so haben Sie die Auswahl zwischen *Dear Sir(s)* bzw. *Dear Madam* und *Dear Sir or Madam*. In diesen Fällen heißt die Schlussformel *Yours faithfully*. Ist das Schreiben an eine weibliche Person gerichtet, die keinen akademischen Titel trägt und von der Sie nicht wissen, ob sie ledig oder verheiratet ist, so lautet die Anrede z.B. *Ms Taylor* (und nicht *Mrs* oder *Miss*).

[2] Wenn Sie regelmäßig mit einem bestimmten Ansprechpartner kommunizieren, so verwenden Sie ruhig *Best wishes* oder *Best regards* als abschließende Formel – diese setzt sich weltweit immer mehr durch.

Musteranschreiben für amerikanische Fachzeitschrift

Musterstraße 1
12345 Musterhausen
Germany
e-mail: peter.muster@abc.de

Professor M.C. Doyle, M.D.　　　　　　　　　　　　5/17/06
Editor-in-Chief of *JOURNAL NAME*
110-114 Sunset Boulevard
Suntown, GA 23450
USA

Dear Professor Doyle:[1]

Please find enclosed our manuscript *"Development of gallstone surgery in Germany 1991–2003: Results of a multicenter survey"*.
This retrospective analysis of 45,500 cholecystectomies describes the changes in diagnostic and therapeutic strategies following the introduction of laparoscopic cholecystectomy. Our work investigates the surgical and non-surgical complication rates, reintervention rates and mortality rates of conventional vs. laparoscopic cholecystectomy with special focus on treatment standards in choledocholithiasis. Our data confirm the outstanding role of the minimally-invasive surgical technique and reveal a clear trend towards endoscopic treatment of bile duct stones.
We believe this manuscript to be of interest to many readers of *JOURNAL NAME* and hope it is suitable for publication.

Sincerely[2]

[signature]

Peter Muster, M.D.

---

[1] Ein Komma anstelle des Doppelpunktes wird als informell angesehen, ist jedoch möglich. Anredekürzel und Titel (*Mr., Ms., Mrs., Dr.*) ziehen im AE immer einen Punkt nach sich. Ist das Schreiben an eine weibliche Person gerichtet, die keinen akademischen Titel trägt und von der Sie nicht wissen, ob sie ledig oder verheiratet ist, so lautet die Anrede z. B. *Ms. Taylor* (und nicht *Mrs.* oder *Miss*). Ist Ihnen der Adressat nicht namentlich bekannt, so verwenden Sie anstelle des britischen *Dear Sirs* die Anrede *Gentlemen*. Als Alternative empfehlen wir das neutrale *Dear Editor(s)*.

[2] Verwenden Sie hier ausschließlich *Sincerely/Sincerely yours/Yours sincerely*.

Optionale Angaben im *cover letter* können Sie wie folgt formulieren:

- Wenn Sie einen *reviewer* vorschlagen möchten:
 As a potential reviewer we would like to suggest Professor M. Smith (Anschrift, E-mail, etc.).

- Wenn Sie ein überarbeitetes Manuskript erneut einsenden:
 Please find enclosed the revised version of "Manuscript Title". We have heeded all of the reviewers' propositions (oder Sie nennen die Namen der *reviewer*, wenn dies nicht zu viele sind). *A detailed response to their comments is attached to this letter* (bei *hard copy* Einsendungen)/*is attached as a separate file* (bei einer *electronic submission*).

 Please find enclosed our manuscript "Manuscript Title", which has been revised according to the reviewers' requests ...

 Please find enclosed our revised manuscript "Manuscript Title" as requested by the reviewers ...

- Wenn Sie eine Eingangsbestätigung wünschen:
 BE: *I (We) should be grateful if you would send me (us) a brief acknowledgement of receipt.*
 AE: *I (We) would appreciate if you sent me (us) a brief acknowledgment of receipt.*
 (Dies erübrigt sich allerdings bei einer *electronic submission*. Darüber hinaus lehnen etliche Redaktionen ein derartiges Verfahren von vornehrein ab.)

- Wenn Sie Bezug zu einer Ihrer bisherigen Publikationen herstellen möchten:
 This research paper is based upon the results of one of our former studies as described in "Muster, P. et al., ...".

Wenn Sie ein Manuskript per *electronic submission* einreichen, ist Ihnen in der Regel vorgegeben, an welcher Stelle Sie die Inhalte des *cover letter* anbringen. Ein Anschreiben im eigentlichen Sinne ist meist nicht mehr notwendig. Viele Zeitschriften bieten ein eigenes Eingabefenster an, wo Sie aufgefordert werden, entsprechende Informationen unmittelbar einzutragen, bzw. einen ausformulierten *cover letter* einzukopieren (*paste*). Ist dies der Fall, so beginnen Sie den einleitenden Satz nach der Anrede mit *Please find attached* (anstatt *Please find enclosed*).

Appendix 2   Comparison AE/BE / Vergleich AE/BE

Einführung

Das heutige Englisch ist geprägt von den beiden großen Varietäten American English (AE) und British English (BE).

Nachstehend finden Sie die wichtigsten Unterschiede zwischen AE und BE, soweit diese für unser Buch relevant erscheinen. Bei der Orthographie haben wir lediglich einige grundlegende Unterschiede aufgelistet. Jedes gute Textverarbeitungsprogramm verfügt über *spell check* und Spracherkennung, so dass die jeweils gewünschte Varietät des Englischen problemlos eingestellt und das Textdokument automatisch auf Rechtschreibfehler hin überprüft werden kann.

1. Aussprache

Ziel unseres Buches ist es, ein grammatikalisch, idiomatisch, sowie kontextuell und situativ korrektes Standardenglisch im naturwissenschaftlichen Bereich zu vermitteln. Aus diesem Grunde wurde auf Lautschrift und Aussprachevariationen verzichtet. Zudem liegt der Schwerpunkt eindeutig auf der Schriftform. Wenn Sie bei einem englischen Vortrag ein Wort falsch betonen oder fehlerhaft aussprechen, so wird Ihnen das der Muttersprachler sicherlich verzeihen.
Zwei Phänomene sollten Sie dennoch bei der Aussprache intus haben:

Der Buchstabe z wird im AE [zi:] gesprochen, im BE [zed].

Wenn Sie im BE Zahlenreihen (beispielsweise eine Telefonnummer) aufsagen, so wird die Null wie der englische Buchstabe *o* gesprochen, im AE hingegen wie die Zahl *zero*.

	AE	BE
3051	three zero five one	three O five one

Nachstehend finden Sie zunächst die wichtigsten Rechtschreiberegeln im Vergleich AE/BE. Auf sprachwissenschaftliche Termini wurde hierbei weitgehend verzichtet. Auf wichtige Unterschiede zwischen AE und BE wird ferner im Buch fortlaufend hingewiesen.

2. Verschiedene Schreibweisen

	AE	BE
Verschiedene Endungen	theater, center	theatre, centre
	honor, color	honour, colour
	defense, offense	defence, offence
	catalog	catalogue
Konsonantendoppelung im BE	traveler, wagon	traveller, waggon
Stummes *e* entfällt oft im AE	acknowledgment, judgment, aging	acknowledgement, judgement, ageing

In Kanada tauchen immer wieder Mischformen bei Verlagen auf, die sich bei einigen Ausdrücken für die amerikanische, bei anderen hingegen für die britische Schreibweise entscheiden (*color* aber *centre*). In vielen Fällen wissen selbst Muttersprachler nicht genau, welches nun die originär britische, bzw. amerikanische Schreibweise ist. In Zeitungstexten – gerade auch an Schnittstellen zwischen den beiden großen englischsprachigen Nationen wie in Kanada oder in Irland – geht es bunt drunter und drüber.
Für Ihr eigenes Manuskript sollten Sie sich abhängig vom Adressaten für eine Variante – AE oder BE – entscheiden, und diese konsequent verfolgen.

Wie sind die folgenden Vergangenheitsformen von Verben einzuordnen?

AE	BE
learned, burned, leaned	learnt, burnt, leant

Bei diesen Beispielen handelt es sich streng genommen nur äußerlich um eine andere Schreibweise; eigentlich geht es hier um regelmäßige Verbformen, welche der Amerikaner bei diesen Verben favorisiert und um unregelmäßige Verbformen, welche der Engländer bevorzugt. Mitunter vermischen sich diese Formen aber auch im AE/BE. Sie sollten lediglich wissen, dass es sie gibt.

Vergleich AE/BE

Es treten stilistisch unterschiedliche Verbformen auf:

AE	BE
We should have gotten more attention.	We should have got more attention.

Die Form *gotten* wird vornehmlich von Amerikanern verwendet und wird in England eher dem Substandard zugeschrieben.

Ein in beiden Sprachen vorhandener Begriff wird unterschiedlich abgekürzt:

AE + BE	AE	BE
advertisement	ad	advert

Verstanden werden selbstverständlich alle drei Formen von beiden Nationalitäten.

Der Gebrauch des bestimmten Artikels *the* ist für deutschsprachige Lernende oft schwer nachvollziehbar und folgt nicht immer klaren Regeln. In vortragstechnischer Hinsicht jedoch ist dies häufig reine Sprachkosmetik. Man wird es Ihnen nachsehen, wenn Sie *the* falsch setzen oder aus Unsicherheit einfach weglassen. Bei wissenschaftlichen Fachausdrücken steht allerdings i.d.R. kein *the* (z.B. *Laparoscopic appendectomy has been widely accepted ...*).

Bei nachstehenden Beispielen steht im AE stets *the*:

AE	BE
The patient was taken to the hospital.	The patient was taken to hospital.
He went to the university. He studied at the university.	He went to university. He studied at university.

Wird die Universität näher bezeichnet, so heißt es sowohl im AE wie im BE *He studied at the University of California*.

Appendix 3   Glossary / Glossar

A

German	English	Pages
Abbildung	figure	40
Abfall	decrease	87, 88
abhängen von	to depend on	79, 80
abhängen von	to relate to	68, 69
ablehnen (etw. a.)	to object to s.th.	75, 76
ablehnen (etw. a.)	to reject s.th.	75, 76
Abnahme	decline	88
abnehmen	to decline	88
abnehmen	to decrease	58, 88
abschätzen	to estimate	60, 61
abschließend	to conclude	77, 97
abschließend	final	92, 93
abschließend	finally	97, 98
abschließend	in conclusion	77
abschließend betrachtet	in a final analysis	98
absegnen	to approve	30
absegnen	to endorse	72, 74
Absicht	intent	11, 12
absinken	to decline	88
abweichen (von)	to deviate (from)	66, 67
abweichen (von)	to vary (from)	66, 67
Abwesenheit (in A. von)	in the absence of	80
ähnlich	similar	55, 65
aktuell	current	92, 93
alle	all (of)	37, 39
alles	all (of)	37, 39
alles in allem	in summary	97
alles in allem	in total	37, 39
alles in allem	on the whole	98
Alter	age	28
am Ende	in conclusion	97, 98
Analyse	analysis	13, 15
analysieren	to analyse	23, 24
andere(s)	another	48
andere(s)	other	48
anderer Meinung sein	to disagree (with)	66, 67
andererseits	on the other hand	54, 56
anders	different	66
anders als	unlike	56
anerkennen	to acknowledge	44, 99, 100
Anerkennung	acknowledgement	99
anfänglich	initial	92, 93
anführen	to name	42

Glossar

German	English	Page
angeben (Daten)	to express (data)	20
annehmen	to assume	83
annehmen	to presume	83
annehmen	to suppose	83
Ansicht	view	85
Ansicht (der A. sein)	to hold the view that …	85
Ansicht (der A. sein)	to suppose	83
Ansicht (unserer A. nach)	in our opinion	85
Ansicht (unserer A. nach)	in our view	85
ansprechen	to address	14
ansteigen	to increase	88
Anstieg	gain	88
Anstieg	increase	87, 88
Anteil	proportion	36, 38
Anteil (prozentualer A.)	percentage	36, 38
Antwortrate	response rate	19, 20
anwenden (einen Test)	to employ (a test)	25
anzeigen	to indicate	63
Arbeit	work	13, 15
Argument (ein A. für etw. liefern)	to provide an argument for s.th.	72, 73
Artikel	article	13, 14
Assistenz	assistance	99, 100
auch	also	48
auf der Hand liegend	evident	70
aufdecken	to disclose	42, 43
aufdecken	to reveal	42, 43
aufgeklärtes Einverständnis	informed consent	30
aufgrund fehlender	in the absence of	80
aufgrund von	because of	68
aufgrund von	due to	68, 69
aufgrund von	owing to	68, 69
auflisten	to list	40
auftreten	to be present	34
auftreten	to be seen	33
auftreten	to occur	34
auftreten (etw. tritt auf)	to encounter (s.th.)	32, 33, 42, 43
Auftreten	occurrence	34
aufwerfen (Bedenken bezüglich etw. a.)	to raise concern about s.th.	76
aufwerfen (Fragen über etw. a.)	to raise questions about s.th.	76
aufwerfen (Zweifel an etw. a.)	to raise doubts about s.th.	76
aufzeichnen	to monitor	21
aufzeichnen	to record	21
aufzeigen	to indicate	41
ausdrücken (Wertschätzung a. gegenüber jmdm.)	to show appreciation (to s.o.)	100
ausgehen (davon a.)	to suppose	83
Ausmaß (von)	extent (of)	90
Ausnahme (von)	exemption (from)	31
ausschließen	to exclude	27

Glossar

Ausschluss	exclusion	26
Ausschlusskriterium	exclusion criterion	26
außerdem	also	48
außerdem	besides	47, 48
außerdem	furthermore	48
außerdem	in addition	47, 48
außerdem	moreover	47, 48
äußerst gründlich	meticulous	94, 95
äußerst sorgfältig	meticulous	94, 95
auswählen	to select	27
Auswahlkriterien	recruitment criteria	27
Auswirkung (auf)	effect (on)	82
Auswirkung (erhebliche A. auf)	impact (on)	82
Auswirkung (geringe A. auf)	bearing (on)	82

B

Bandbreite	gamut	32, 35
Bandbreite	scale	32, 35
basieren auf	to be based on	79, 80
beabsichtigen	to aim	11
beabsichtigen	to be intended to	12
beabsichtigen	to set out to	12
beantworten (eine Frage eindeutig b.)	to settle a question	16
bedenken	to acknowledge	44
bedenken	to consider	43
Bedenken bezüglich etw. aufwerfen	to raise concern about s.th.	76
bedeutend	significant	53
bedingen	to contribute to	71
bedingt sein durch	to relate to	68, 69
beeindruckend	impressive	53
beeinflussen	to affect	79, 82
beeinflussen	to influence	79, 82
befassen (sich besonders mit etw. b.)	to focus on s.th.	95
befassen (sich mit etw. b.)	to concern oneself with s.th.	16
Befragter	respondent	19, 20
befürworten	to advocate	72, 74
befürworten	to approve of s.th.	74
befürworten	to endorse	72, 74
befürworten	to favour s.th.	74
befürworten (nicht b.)	to disapprove of	75
begegnen	to come across s.th.	33
begegnen (etw. b.)	to encounter (s.th.)	32, 33, 42, 43
begleitet werden von	to be accompanied by	80
begründet durch	caused by	68, 69
begrüßen	to approve of s.th.	74
behaupten	to assert	85
behaupten	to claim	63, 85
behaupten	to contend	85

Glossar

behaupten	to maintain	85
Beilage (Informations-B.)	supplementary information	19, 21
Beispiel	example	49
Beispiel (zum B.)	e.g.	49
Beispiel (zum B.)	for example	49
Beispiel (zum B.)	for instance	49
Beistand	assistance	99, 100
beitragen zu	to contribute to	71
bekannt machen	to disclose	42, 43
bekräftigen	to confirm	72, 73
bekräftigen	to corroborate	72, 73
Belang	concern	16
belaufen (sich b. auf)	to stand at	35
bemerken	to mention	42
bemerken	to perceive	42, 43
bemerkenswert	remarkable	51, 52
beobachten	to monitor	21
beobachten	to observe	32, 33, 42, 43
beobachten	to see	33
berechnen	to calculate	23, 24
Bericht	report	13, 14
berichten	to report	42, 43, 62
Berücksichtigung (unter B. von)	with respect to	79, 81
beschreiben	to describe	14, 45, 62
besondere(-n/-s)	special	53
besonders	particular	51, 52
besonders	particularly	52
besonders	special	53
bestätigen	to confirm	72, 73
bestätigen	to prove	72, 73
bestimmen	to determine	15, 23, 24
betonen	to emphasize	51
betonen	to stress	51
betonen	to underscore	52
Betracht (in B. ziehen)	to take into account	44
Betracht (in B. ziehen)	to take into consideration	43
betrachten (etw. genauer b.)	to take a closer look at s.th.	94, 95
beträchtlich	considerable	51, 52, 90
beurteilen	to assess	16, 23, 24, 60
beurteilen	to evaluate	15, 23, 24, 60
beurteilen (etw. auf etw. hin b.)	to assess s.th. for s.th.	60
beweisen	to prove	72, 73
bewerten	to assess	16, 23, 60
bewerten	to evaluate	15, 23, 60
Bewertung	assessment	61
beziehungsweise	respectively	35
Bezug zu	bearing on	82
bezüglich etw. untersuchen	to screen (for)	21
bezuschussen	to fund	99, 101

Glossar

bieten (Unterstützung b.)	to provide support for s.th.	72, 74
billigen	to lend countenance to	74
bis jetzt	so far	93
bis jetzt	thus far	93
bisher	to date	92, 93
bislang	to date	92, 93
bringen (jmdm. gegenüber Dankbarkeit zum Ausdruck b.)	to express gratitude to s.o.	100
bringen (mit sich b.)	to be associated with	79
Bruchteil	fraction	36, 38

D

Dank an jmdn. richten	to address thanks to s.o.	100
Dank an jmdn. richten	to extend thanks to s.o.	100
Dank gebührt jmdm.	thanks are due to s.o.	100
dankbar sein	to be grateful to	99, 100
Dankbarkeit (jmdm. gegenüber D. zum Ausdruck bringen)	to express gratitude to s.o.	100
danken	to thank	99
danken (jmdm. d.)	to address thanks to s.o.	100
danken (jmdm. d.)	to extend thanks to s.o.	100
dankend (jmdn. d. erwähnen)	to show appreciation to s.o.	100
Danksagung	acknowledgements	99
dann	then	47
darbieten	to give	41
darlegen	to report	41
darstellen	to depict	45
darstellen	to represent	35
darstellen (plakativ d.)	to delineate	45
darüber hinaus	besides	47, 48
darüber hinaus	furthermore	48
darüber hinaus	in addition	47, 48
darüber hinaus	moreover	47, 48
darum	that is (the reason) why	71
Daten	data	19
Daten erheben über etw.	to collect (data about s.th.)	22
davon ausgehen	to suppose	83
definieren (als)	to define (as)	28
demonstrieren	to demonstrate	41, 63, 72, 73
dennoch	yet	54, 57
dennoch	nevertheless	57
dennoch	nonetheless	57
der Ansicht sein	to suppose	83
deshalb	hence	71
deshalb	therefore	71
deswegen	hence	71, 77, 78
deswegen	therefore	71, 77, 78
deswegen	that is (the reason) why	71

Glossar

deswegen	thus	77, 78
Detail (ins D. gehen)	to go into detail	94
detailliert	detailed	94
detailliert	in detail	94
detailliert erläutern (etw. d.e.)	to detail (s.th.)	94
Diagramm	diagram	40, 41
differenzieren (zwischen)	to differentiate (between)	54, 55
dokumentieren	to report	62
Drittel (ein D. von)	(one) third (of)	36, 39
drittens	third	47
durchführen	to perform	25
durchführen (eine Studie)	to conduct (a study)	13
durchführen (eine Studie)	to perform (a study)	13
durchführen (einen Test)	to perform (a test)	24

E

ein paar	a few	36, 37
Einblick in etw. gewähren	to offer insight into s.th.	16
eindeutig	clear	70
einerseits	on the one hand	54, 56
Einfluss (auf)	effect (on)	82
Einfluss (starker E. auf)	impact (on)	82
eingehend	exhaustive	94, 95
einige	a few	36, 37
einnehmen (eine unterschiedliche Haltung e.)	to take a different view on	66
einreichen	to submit	20
einschätzen	to assess	16, 23, 24, 60
einschätzen	to evaluate	15, 23, 24, 60
einschließen	to comprise	27
einschließen	to enlist	27
einschließen	to enrol	27
einschließen	to include	26
Einschluss	inclusion	26
Einschlusskriterium	inclusion criterion	26
einstufen (als)	to classify (as)	28
einteilen (in Kategorien)	to group	28
einverstanden sein (nicht e.s.)	to disagree (with)	75
Einverständnis (aufgeklärtes E.)	informed consent	30
endgültig	final	92, 93
entdecken	to detect	33, 42, 43
entgegen	contrary to	56
entscheidend	critical	53
entscheidend	crucial	53
entscheidend (alles e.)	vital	53
entscheidend (alles e.)	paramount	53
entsprechen	to correspond with	64
entsprechen	to represent	35
Entwicklung	development	58

Glossar

erachten (etw. für etw. e.)	to believe s.th. (to be) s.th.	61
erachten (etw. für etw. e.)	to consider s.th. (to be) s.th.	61
erachten (etw. für etw. e.)	to deem s.th. (as) s.th.	61
erachten (etw. für etw. e.)	to regard s.th. as s.th.	61
Erfahrung (nach unserer E.)	in our experience	86
erfordern	to require	31
erforschen	to explore	15
erforschen (genauestens e.)	to scrutinize	95
erfragen	to query	20
Ergebnis	finding	32, 33
Ergebnis	outcome	32, 33
Ergebnis	result	32, 33
Ergebnis (im E.)	as a result	78
Ergebnis (zu einem E. kommen)	to find	32, 33
erhalten (etw. e.)	to obtain s.th.	22
erheben (Daten e. über etw.)	to collect (data about s.th.)	22
erhebliche Auswirkung auf	impact (on)	82
Erhebung	survey	13, 14
erhöhen um	to increase by	59
erklären	to explain	71
erklären (sich e. durch)	to be explained by	71
Erklärung	explanation	71
erlangen (Kenntnis e. über etw.)	to gain knowledge of s.th.	22
erläutern (etw. detailliert e.)	to detail (s.th.)	94
erläutern (etw. genauer e.)	to detail (s.th.)	94
erniedrigen um	to decrease by	59
erschöpfend	exhaustive	94, 95
erstens	first	47
erstens	firstly	47
erstens	first off	47
erstere(s)	the former	48
erstmalig	for the first time	17
erwägen	to consider	43
Erwägung (in E. ziehen)	to take into account	44
Erwägung (in E. ziehen)	to take into consideration	43
erwähnen	to mention	42
erwähnen	to report	42, 43
erwähnen (jmdn. dankend e.)	to show appreciation to s.o.	100
Essay	essay	13, 15
essenziell	essential	53
Ethikkommission	ethical committee	30, 31

F

Fachaufsatz	essay	13, 15
favorisieren	to favour s.th.	74
feststellen	to detect	33, 42, 43
feststellen	to determine	15
feststellen	to find	62

Glossar

German	English	Pages
feststellen	to identify	34
feststellen	to observe	42, 43
feststellen	to reveal	34, 42, 43
finanziell unterstützen	to fund	99, 101
finden	to find	32, 33, 62
folglich	as a consequence	68, 70, 77, 78
folglich	in conclusion	77
folglich	thus	77, 78
Follow-Up	follow-up	19, 21
fördern	to enhance	59
Forschung	research	13, 16
Frage (eine F. eindeutig beantworten)	to settle a question	16
Frage (etw. in F. stellen)	to challenge s.th.	76
Frage (etw. in F. stellen)	to question s.th.	76
Fragebogen	questionnaire	19, 20
Fragen über etw. aufwerfen	to raise questions about s.th.	76
Freistellung (von)	exemption (from)	31
früher	previous	92
für etw. sein	to be in favour of s.th.	74

G

German	English	Pages
gegen etw. sein	to be against s.th.	75
Gegensatz (im G. zu)	contrary to	56
Gegensatz (im G. zu)	in contrast to	66, 67
Gegensatz (im G. zu)	opposed to	54, 56
Gegenstand	subject	26
Gegenteil (im G.)	on the contrary	54, 56
gegenteilig	contradictory	56, 66, 67
gegenüberstehen (einem Problem g.)	to face a problem	96
gegenüberstellen	to contrast	54, 56
gegenwärtig	current	92, 93
gegenwärtig	present	92, 93
gehen (ins Detail g.)	to go into detail	94
genauestens erforschen	to scrutinize	95
genauestens untersuchen	to scrutinize	95
genauer erläutern (etw. g.e.)	to detail (s.th.)	94
genehmigen	to approve	30
genehmigen	to endorse	72, 74
gering	minor	87
geringe Auswirkung auf	bearing (on)	82
geringfügig	marginal	89
geringfügig	slight	89
geringfügig	slightly	89
gesamt	total	37, 39
Gesamt-	overall	37, 39
Gesamtheit	overall	29
Gesamtheit	total	28, 37, 39
Gesamtzahl	overall	29

Glossar

Gesamtzahl	total	28
gewähren (Einblick in etw. g.)	to offer insight into s.th.	16
gewinnen	to obtain	22
gewinnen (Informationen g. über etw.)	to gather (information about s.th.)	22
glauben	to believe	86
gleich	identical	55
gleichzeitig mit	in tandem with	80
Grad	degree	90
gravierend	crucial	53
Grenzen (an G. stoßen)	to encounter limitations	96
groß	vast	90
größtenteils	for the most part	89
größtenteils	largely	87, 89
Grund (aus diesem G.)	for this reason	71
Grund (aus diesem G.)	that is (the reason) why	71
gründlich	thorough	94, 95
gründlich (äußerst g.)	meticulous	94, 95
Gruppe	group	28
gruppieren	to group	28
gutheißen	to endorse	31, 72, 74

H

Hälfte (die H. von)	half (of)	36, 38
halten (etw. für etw. h.)	to believe s.th. (to be) s.th.	61
halten (etw. für etw. h.)	to consider s.th. (to be) s.th.	61
halten (etw. für etw. h.)	to deem s.th. (as) s.th.	61
halten (etw. für etw. h.)	to regard s.th. as s.th.	61
Haltung (eine unterschiedliche H. einnehmen)	to take a different view on	66
Hand (auf der H. liegend)	evident	70
häufig	frequent	87, 88
häufig	frequently	88
Häufigkeit	frequency	32, 34, 88
Häufigkeit	rate	32, 34
Haupt-	main	87, 89
Haupt-	major	87
hauptsächlich	main	87, 89
hauptsächlich	mainly	87, 89
hauptsächlich	major	87
hegen (Zweifel an etw. h.)	to harbour doubts about s.th.	76
heranziehen	to retrieve	21
herausfinden	to find	32, 33
herausragend	paramount	53
herrühren von	to originate from	68, 69
herrühren von	to stem from	68, 69
hervorheben	to foreground	51
hervorheben	to highlight	41, 51, 52
Hilfe	help	99

Glossar

Hinblick (im H. auf)	with regard to	79, 81
Hinblick (im H. auf)	with respect to	79, 81
hingegen	however	54, 57
Hinsicht (in dieser H.)	in this respect	81
hinsichtlich	concerning	81
hinsichtlich	in respect of	81
hinweisen	to indicate	63, 71, 72
hinweisen (auf)	to point out	51
hinweisen auf	to indicate	72, 73, 78
hoch	high	36, 37

I

identisch	identical	55
illustrieren	to illustrate	14, 15
im Ergebnis	as a result	78
im Gegensatz zu	contrary to	56
im Gegensatz zu	in contrast to	66, 67
im Gegensatz zu	opposed to	54, 56
im Gegenteil	on the contrary	54, 56
im Hinblick auf	with regard to	79, 81
im Hinblick auf	with respect to	79, 81
im Vergleich (dazu)	in comparison	55
im Widerspruch zu	in contrast to	56
in Abwesenheit von	in the absence of	80
in Betracht ziehen	to take into account	44
in Betracht ziehen	to take into consideration	43
in dieser Hinsicht	in this respect	81
in Übereinstimmung mit	in accordance with	64
in Übereinstimmung mit	in agreement with	64, 65
in Übereinstimmung mit	in keeping with	64, 65
in Übereinstimmung mit	in line with	64, 65
in Verbindung mit	in conjunction with	80
Individuen	individuals	26
Informationen (I. gewinnen über etw.)	to gain information about s.th.	22
ins Detail gehen	to go into detail	94
insbesondere	in particular	52
insgesamt	in total	28
insgesamt	overall	29, 39, 97, 98
intensiv	intensive	94, 95
Interesse (von I.)	question of interest	16
Inzidenz	incidence	32, 34

J

jedoch	however	54, 57

K

Kenntnis erlangen über etw.	to gain knowledge of s.th.	22
klar	clear	70
klassifizieren	to classify	28
Kohorte	cohort	26, 27
kommen (zu einem Ergebnis k.)	to find	32, 33
komplett	total	37, 39
konkordant mit	concordant with	64, 65
konzentrieren (sich auf etw. k.)	to focus on s.th.	95
korrelieren mit	to correlate with	64
kritisieren	to criticize	75
kürzlich	recent	92

L

lebenswichtig	vital	53
letztere(s)	the latter	48
letztlich	finally	47, 48
liefern	to provide	20
liefern (ein Argument für etw. l.)	to provide an argument for s.th.	72, 73
limitiert sein (durch)	to be limited by	96
Limitierung	limitation	96
Lupe (unter die L. nehmen)	to scrutinize	45, 46

M

manche	some	36, 37
marginal	marginal	89
maximieren	to maximize	91
mehr	more	87
Mehrheit	majority	36, 39
meiner festen Überzeugung nach	it is my contention that	86
Meinung	opinion	85
Meinung (anderer M. sein)	to disagree (with)	66, 67
Meinung (unserer M. nach)	in our opinion	85
Meinung (unserer M. nach)	in our view	85
messen	to measure	21
Methode	method	19, 20
Minderheit	minority	37, 39
mindern um	to decrease by	59
minimieren	to minimize	91
missbilligen (etw. m.)	to disapprove of (s.th.)	75
mit etw. zusammenhängen	to be associated with (s.th.)	79
mit sich bringen	to be associated with	79
multifaktoriell	multifactorial	70

Glossar

N

nachbeobachten (etw. n.)	to follow (s.th.) up	21
nach unserer Erfahrung	in our experience	86
Nachbeobachtung	follow-up	19, 21
Nachweis von etw.	evidence of s.th.	34
neben	besides	48
nehmen (unter die Lupe n.)	to scrutinize	45, 46
nennen	to name	42
neu	new	17
neuartig	novel	17
nicht befürworten	to disapprove of	75
nicht einverstanden sein	to disagree (with)	75
nicht zustimmen	to disagree (with)	67
nichts	none (of)	37, 39
niedrig	low	36, 37
niemand	none (of)	37, 39

O

offensichtlich	apparent	70
offensichtlich	evident	70
offensichtlich	obvious	70
ohne	in the absence of	80

P

paar (ein p.)	a few	36, 37
parallel	in tandem with	80
Patientenauswahl	patient selection	27
Patientenkollektiv	patient population	27
Patientenpopulation	patient population	27
Person	subject	26
plakativ darstellen	to delineate	45
präsentieren	to present	14, 41
Problem	problem	96
Problem (einem P. gegenüberstehen)	to face a problem	96
Problem (mit einem P. konfrontiert werden)	to be faced with a problem	96
Prozentsatz	percentage	36, 38
prozentualer Anteil	percentage	36, 38
prüfen	to test	15

R

randomisiert zuteilen	to randomise	28
Rat	advice	99, 100
Rate	rate	32, 34, 36, 38
Reduktion	decrease	87, 88
reichen (von ... bis ... r.)	to range (from ... to ...)	32, 35, 90

Glossar

Deutsch	Englisch	Seite
Reihe	series	26, 27
Reihe (eine R. von)	a number of	36, 37
Reihe (eine R. von)	a score of	36, 37
Reihe (von Probanden)	cohort	26, 27
rekrutieren	to enlist	27
rekrutieren	to enrol	27
rekrutieren	to recruit	27
Resultat	result	32, 33
resultieren aus	to result from	68, 69
richten (Dank an jmdn. r.)	to address thanks to s.o.	100
richten (Dank an jmdn. r.)	to extend thanks to s.o.	100
Rücklaufquote	rate of return	19, 20

S

Deutsch	Englisch	Seite
schätzen	to estimate	60, 61, 83, 84
Schätzung	estimate	60, 61
schildern	to delineate	45
schließlich	finally	47, 48, 97
schließlich	in conclusion	97, 98
Schluss	finding	32, 33
schlussfolgern	to conclude	77
Schlussfolgerung	conclusion	77
schwanken (von ... bis ... s.)	to vary (from ... to ...)	90
Schwankungsbreite	variation	91
schwerwiegend	major	87
sein (der Ansicht s.)	to hold the view that ...	85
sein (der Ansicht s.)	to suppose	83
sein (für etw. s.)	to be in favour of s.th.	74
sein (gegen etw. s.)	to be against s.th.	75
selten	rare	87, 88
selten	rarely	87, 89
Serie	series	26, 27
signifikant	significant	23, 53
Signifikanz	significance	23, 24
sinken	to decline	88
somit	in conclusion	77
sorgfältig (äußerst s.)	meticulous	94, 95
Spektrum	gamut	32, 35
Spektrum	scale	32, 35
sporadisch	rare	87, 88
sporadisch	rarely	89
starker Einfluss auf	impact (on)	82
steigern	to enhance	59
steigern (um)	to increase (by)	59, 88
Steigerung	increase	87, 88
Stichprobe	sample	26
stoßen (an Grenzen stoßen)	to encounter limitations	96
stoßen (auf etw.)	to come across s.th.	33

Glossar

Studie	study	13
Studienprotokoll	study protocol	19, 20

T

Tabelle	table	40
Teil	part	36, 38
Teil (zu einem großen T.)	in large part	89
Teil (zum größten T.)	for the most part	89
teilnehmen (an etw. t.)	to participate (in s.th.)	27
teilnehmen (an etw. t.)	to take part (in s.th.)	27
teilweise	partial	36, 38
Tendenz	tendency	58
testen	to test	15, 23, 24
Thema	subject	26
tiefschürfend	thorough	94, 95
tragend	critical	53
Tragweite	extent	90
treffen (eine Unterscheidung t.)	to make a distinction	56
trotz	despite	57
trotz	in spite of	57
trotzdem	nevertheless	57
trotzdem	nonetheless	57

U

Überblick	survey	13, 14
Überblick geben (einen Ü. geben über etw.)	to review	14
übereinstimmen mit	to be consistent with	64
übereinstimmend mit	concordant with	64, 65
Übereinstimmung (in Ü. mit)	in accordance with	64
Übereinstimmung (in Ü. mit)	in agreement with	64, 65
Übereinstimmung (in Ü. mit)	in keeping with	64, 65
Übereinstimmung (in Ü. mit)	in line with	64, 65
überschätzen	to overestimate	60, 83, 84
Übersicht	survey	13, 14
Übersichtsarbeit	review	13, 14
übersteigen	to exceed	91
übertreffen	to exceed	91
überwiegend	largely	87, 89
überwiegend	vast	90
überzeugt sein, dass ...	to be convinced that	85
überzeugt sein (von etw. ü.)	to be convinced (of s.th.)	85
Überzeugung (meiner festen Ü. nach)	it is my contention that	86
um zu	in order to	12
umfassend	extensive	94, 95
unabhängig von	independent of	80
unbedeutendes Detail (ein u.D.)	a minute detail	95

Glossar

German	English	Page
ungeachtet	regardless of	81
unserer Ansicht nach	in our opinion	85
unserer Ansicht nach	in our view	85
unserer Meinung nach	in our opinion	85
unserer Meinung nach	in our view	85
unter Berücksichtigung von	with respect to	79, 81
unter die Lupe nehmen	to scrutinize	45, 46
Untergruppe	subgroup	28
untermauern	to corroborate	72, 73
unterschätzen	to underestimate	60, 83, 84
unterscheiden (sich u. von)	to differ from	66, 67
unterscheiden (zwischen)	to distinguish (between)	54, 55
Unterscheidung (eine U. treffen) (zwischen)	to make a distinction (between)	56
unterschiedlich	different	66
unterstreichen	to underline	51, 52
unterstreichen	to underscore	52
unterstützen	to lend countenance to	74
unterstützen	to support	72, 73, 99, 101
unterstützen (finanziell u.)	to fund	99, 101
Unterstützung	assistance	99, 101
Unterstützung	support	99
Unterstützung bieten	to provide support for s.th.	72, 74
untersuchen	to examine	15, 23, 25
untersuchen	to explore	15
untersuchen	to investigate	15
untersuchen (auf etw. hin u.)	to screen (for)	21
untersuchen (bezüglich etw. u.)	to screen (for)	21
untersuchen (genauestens u.)	to scrutinize	95
Untersuchung	investigation	13, 15
Untersuchung (eine eingehende U.)	a closer examination	95

V

German	English	Page
Variabilität	variability	90
Variabilität	variation	91
variieren (von ... bis... v.)	to vary (from ... to ...)	32, 35, 90
veranschaulichen	to illustrate	14
verantwortlich (für)	responsible (for)	71
verarbeiten	to process	25
verbessern	to enhance	59
verbessern (sich v.)	to improve	58, 59
Verbindung (in V. mit)	in conjunction with	80
verdeutlichen	to highlight	41
verdeutlichen	to illustrate	45
verdeutlichen	to specify	45, 46
verfechten	to contend	85
verfügbar	available	20

Glossar

Verfügung (zur V. stehen)	available	20
Verfügung (zur V. stellen)	to submit	20
vergangen	past	92
Vergangenheit	past	92
Vergleich (im V.)	in comparison	55
vergleichbar	comparable	55, 65
vergleichbar (etw. ist gut mit etw. v.)	s.th. compares favourably with s.th.	65
vergleichen	to compare	23, 41
vergleichen (etw. mit etw. v.)	to compare (s.th. with s.th.)	16, 25, 54
Vergleichsarbeit	comparison study	63
Vergleichsstudie	comparison study	63
Verhältnis	proportion	36, 38
vermuten	to assume	83
vermuten	to presume	83
vermuten	to suggest	83, 84
vermuten lassen	to suggest	83, 84
Vermutung	assumption	83
vernachlässigen (zu v.)	marginal	89
verschärfen	to exacerbate	59
verschlechtern	to exacerbate	59
verschlechtern (sich v.)	to deteriorate	58, 59
verstärken	to enhance	59
versuchen	to attempt	12
verursacht von	caused by	68, 69
verursacht werden durch	to be related to	79
verwenden	to use	24
verwenden (einen Test)	to use a test	24
verzeichnen	to cite	62
verzeichnen	to note	62
verzeichnen	to record	21
verzichten (auf)	to waive	31
viele	many	36, 37
Vielfalt	variability	90
Viertel (ein V. von)	(one) quarter (of)	36
von Interesse	question of interest	16
vor allem	above all	51, 52
vorbringen	to suggest	63
vorhergehend	previous	92
vorliegend	present	92, 93
vorstellen	to present	14
vorwiegend	predominantly	89

W

wahrnehmen	to perceive	42, 43
was etw. angeht	as far as s.th. is concerned	82
was etw. angeht	as for s.th.	81

Glossar

was etw. angeht	in terms of	81
wegen	because of	68
wegen	due to	68, 69
wegen	owing to	68, 69
weil	because of	68,
weitere(s)	another	48
weitere(s)	other	48
weitreichend	extensive	90, 94
wenig	little	36, 37
wenige	few	36, 37
weniger	less	87, 88
Wertschätzung ausdrücken (gegenüber jmdm.)	to show appreciation (to s.o.)	100
wesentlich	essential	53
wichtig	important	51, 52
widerlegen (etw. w.)	to disprove s.th.	75, 76
widerspiegeln	to reflect	41
widersprechen	to contradict	66, 67
widersprechen	to object to s.th.	75, 76
widersprechend	contradictory	56, 66, 67
Widerspruch (im W. zu)	in contrast to	56
wie etwa	like	49
wie etwa	such as	49, 50
wie z.B.	like	49
wie z.B.	such as	49, 50
winziges Detail (ein w. D.)	a minute detail	95
wogegen	whereas	56
würdigen	to acknowledge	99, 100

Z

zeigen	to demonstrate	41, 63, 72, 73
zeigen	to give	41
zeigen	to indicate	78
zeigen	to present	41
zeigen	to show	40, 62, 72
zeigen (sich z.)	to reveal	34
Zeitraum	period	19, 21
Ziel	aim	11
Ziel	goal	11
Ziel	objective	11
ziehen (in Betracht z.)	to take into account	44
ziehen (in Betracht z.)	to take into consideration	43
zu einem großen Teil	in large part	89
zu einem Ergebnis kommen	to find	32, 33
zu vernachlässigen	marginal	89
Zukunft	future	92, 93

Glossar

Deutsch	Englisch	Seite
zukünftig	future	92, 93
zum Beispiel	e.g.	49
zum Beispiel	for example	49
zum Beispiel	for instance	49
zum ersten Mal	for the first time	17
zum größten Teil	for the most part	89
zunehmen	to increase	58
zur Verfügung stehen	available	20
zur Verfügung stellen	to submit	20
zurückweisen	to reject s. th	75, 76
zurückführen auf	to attribute to	68, 70
zurückzuführen auf	attributable to	68, 70
zusammen	in total	37, 39
zusammen mit	along with	80
zusammen mit	coupled with	80
zusammen mit	in conjunction with	80
zusammen mit	together with	80
zusammenfassen	to sum up	97
zusammenfassen	to summarize	41, 97
zusammenfassend	to sum up	97
zusammenfassend	summing up	97
zusammenfügen	to combine	41
zusammengefasst	in summary	97
Zusammenhang	context	79, 81
zusammenhängen mit	to be related to	79
zusammenhängen mit	to relate to	68, 69
zusammenhängen (mit etw. z.)	to be associated with (s.th.)	79
zusammensetzen (sich z. aus)	to consist (of)	27
zusammenwirken	to combine (to)	71
zustimmen	to approve	30
zustimmen	to endorse	31
zustimmen (nicht z.)	to disagree (with)	66, 67
Zustimmung	approval	30, 31
zuteilen (randomisiert z.)	to randomise	28
Zweck	purpose	11, 12
Zweifel an etw. aufwerfen	to raise doubts about s.th.	76
Zweifel an etw. hegen	to harbour doubts about s.th.	76
zweitens	second	47